Regency Spies

For Nigel, Lizzie and Gareth

Regency Spies

Secret Histories of Britain's Rebels and Revolutionaries

Sue Wilkes

PEN & SWORD
HISTORY

First published in Great Britain in 2015 by
Pen & Sword History
an imprint of
Pen & Sword Books Ltd
47 Church Street
Barnsley
South Yorkshire
S70 2AS

ISBN 978 1 78340 061 4

Typeset in Ehrhardt by
Mac Style Ltd, Bridlington, East Yorkshire
Printed and bound in the UK by CPI Group (UK) Ltd,
Croydon, CRO 4YY

Pen & Sword Books Ltd incorporates the imprints of Pen & Sword
Archaeology, Atlas, Aviation, Battleground, Discovery, Family
History, History, Maritime, Military, Naval, Politics, Railways, Select,
Transport, True Crime, and Fiction, Frontline Books, Leo Cooper,
Praetorian Press, Seaforth Publishing and Wharncliffe.

For a complete list of Pen & Sword titles please contact
PEN & SWORD BOOKS LIMITED
47 Church Street, Barnsley, South Yorkshire, S70 2AS, England
E-mail: enquiries@pen-and-sword.co.uk
Website: www.pen-and-sword.co.uk

Contents

Acknowledgements

I have many people to thank for their help and encouragement. I am extremely grateful to Eloise Hansen, Michelle Higgs, Simon Fowler, Jen Newby, and Roy and Lesley Adkins.

I would like to thank the Library of Congress's Head of Reference Section, Prints and Photographs Division, Barbara Natanson, for her help regarding illustrations, Graeme Siddall, the Archive and Heritage Assistant at Sheffield City Council, Libraries Archives and Information, and Lynette Cawthra, Library Manager at the Working Class Movement Library.

Quotations from the 4th Earl Fitzwilliam papers, WWM/F (Wentworth Woodhouse) are reproduced by kind permission from The Milton (Peterborough) Estates Company and the Director of Communities, Sheffield City Council. (The Wentworth Woodhouse papers have been accepted in lieu of Inheritance Tax by HM Government and allocated to Sheffield City Council).

Any errors are the author's own. Every effort has been made to trace copyright holders for images used in this work. The publishers welcome information on any attributions which may have been omitted.

Last but not least, I must thank my husband Nigel, and my children Elizabeth and Gareth, for their help and support as I disappeared for several months into Regency times yet again.

Abbreviations

LCS	London Corresponding Society
SCCLAI	Sheffield City Council, Libraries Archives and Information
SSCI	Sheffield Society for Constitutional Information
SCI	Society of Constitutional Information
UE	United Englishmen
UI	United Irishmen
WCML	Working Class Movement Library

Introduction

Friar-Gate Gaol, Derby

Friday, 7 November 1817: 11.45 am

For Jeremiah Brandreth, William Turner and Isaac Ludlam, time is running out...

Several thousand people are crammed into the street outside the county gaol. Special constables surround a newly-erected scaffold and gallows of ingenious design, from which all three men will hang simultaneously. Sheriff's officials on horseback, armed with javelins, line the back of the scaffold; dragoons are stationed at both ends of the street. No-one knows if there will be a last-minute rescue attempt.

The doomed men wait to mount the scaffold and suffer the ultimate penalty for high treason. 'Jerry' Brandreth, the so-called 'Nottingham Captain', stares coolly at the immense crowd. He declares in a loud, firm voice, "God be with you all, and Lord Castlereagh too!" Jerry stands quietly, resolutely, as the executioner removes the black silk handkerchief from around his neck and replaces it with a noose.

William Turner is next. As the rope slips around his neck, he shouts: "This is all Oliver and the government! The Lord have mercy on my soul!"[1] The prison chaplain swiftly interrupts and positions himself between the two prisoners and the crowd. The authorities dare not risk any more political controversy.

Isaac Ludlam is last to climb the scaffold. His final moments seem to be spent in fervent prayer, but the chaplain prays so loudly that the traitor's voice cannot be heard by the crowd. After the prisoners have recited the Lord's Prayer, the executioner places a cap over each man's head.

At 12.35 pm the men are hanged. Brandreth and Turner's sufferings are soon over, but Ludlam kicks and struggles for several minutes before his body grows still. The three men are left dangling for half an hour to ensure that life is extinct; then the executioner fetches two axes and two knives. He cuts down Brandreth, removes the cap from his head, and puts his body on a block; a basket is placed beneath Jerry's head. The hangman tries to sever the head with his axe, but uses insufficient force. The crowd jeers and groans with horror. The hangman's assistant finishes off the grisly task with a knife – and Jerry's head drops into the waiting basket.

The hangman picks up the blood-smeared head by its hair and shows it to the multitude: "Behold the head of the traitor Jeremiah Brandreth!" The crowd screams and scatters; some dragoons draw their swords. But the people melt away without incident. Few wait to see the hangman perform the same ghastly ritual with Turner and Ludlam.[2]

'This is all Oliver and the government!' William Turner's last words referred to Oliver – just one member of the British government's shadowy network of spies and informers who kept watch on the nation's underprivileged masses during the late Georgian era.

At that time Britain was under threat at home and abroad. The French Revolution of 1789 shook the world. The crowned heads of Europe no longer slept soundly in their beds following the overthrow and grisly execution of Louis XVI and his wife Marie Antoinette. France's new rulers purged the nation of aristocrats and political enemies in a deadly 'Reign of Terror'. The French nation's church, constitution and state were overturned, and even the days and months of the calendar were rewritten.

France's blood-soaked Revolution was fuelled by social injustice. In Britain, too, there was a huge gulf between rich and poor. The Prince of Wales received £60,000 per year from the Civil List in 1798, while a Stockport cotton weaver earned about £56 annually.[3] Dissenters and Roman Catholics faced stringent restrictions on their education and employment and were forbidden to hold public office. In Ireland the (mainly Catholic) peasantry suffered appalling hardships under British rule.

Memories of the 1780 Gordon Riots still loomed large in people's minds; London had burned and 'King Mob' rampaged for several days, following an attempt to ease restrictions on Roman Catholics. The lower orders feared a return to the days of absolute monarchy; economic hardship also played a part in their anger.

The upper and middle classes were haunted by the thought that their social inferiors might follow the example of the French peasantry when times were hard. The dramatist Frederick Reynolds (1764–1841) recalled that: 'The revolutionary mania daily increasing... thousands in England became *alarmists*'. Reynolds was terrified that a 'revolutionary army' would soon 'march to London, seize the Bank, stop our dividends, and poverty, famine and despair' would reign.[4]

The government was determined to ensure that no revolution would take place in Britain. Even moderate, peaceful reformers were regarded by the authorities as potential rebels. One experienced London magistrate labelled local 'debating societies' as 'vehicles of sedition'.[5] Any hint of political dissent was ruthlessly suppressed.

The true extent of the threat of revolution in mainland Britain has been hotly disputed by historians. The problem lies with the nature of the surviving historical records. The primary evidence comprises hundreds of Home Office files preserved by The National Archives, plus related correspondence and family papers held locally. The records include letters between Whitehall and local magistrates, ministerial correspondence, spy reports, heads of evidence against prisoners awaiting trial, witness statements, prisoners' confessions, treasury solicitor papers, etc.

Unfortunately, much evidence relating to the revolutionary threat has been destroyed or lost, either by contemporaries or during the Victorian era. It appears that some Home Office files were weeded out by officials at an unknown date. Spy reports have been censored – the spies' names have been snipped from the documents or rendered illegible with ink blots. A number of documents survive only in the form of copies or brief extracts. In addition, the papers of the Duke of Portland (Home Secretary from 1794 until 1801) dating from 1780 onwards were all burnt by a family member after his death,[6] although this was not necessarily for sinister reasons – bonfires of personal documents were apparently fairly common.

Some primary evidence of criminal activities never saw the light of day. We know from spy reports that conspirators often burnt letters as soon as they had read the contents – and others were too clever to write down anything that could potentially hang them.

At first glance, the spies' own evidence must be regarded as suspect. A spy may have inflated or exaggerated the seriousness of the events he reported, supplying his employers with sensational stories in order to stay on the state payroll. However, the authorities went to great lengths to ensure that the information they received was accurate. They cross-checked spy reports against other sources whenever possible. An informant who proved unreliable was swiftly axed, if only for reasons of economy – employing spies was an expensive business.

These gaps in the historical record make it extremely difficult to give a definitive answer to the controversy surrounding the true extent of the revolutionary underground, or even confirm whether or not one existed. Nevertheless, the government of the day certainly believed that the danger was real, and their actions must be judged accordingly.

Regency Spies is an attempt to portray the workings of the spy system, and the threat to society at home, from the Regency crisis of 1788–9 until the accession of George IV in 1820. It concentrates on the home-grown revolutionaries, Radicals and workers whose thoughts, words and deeds seemingly imperilled the established order. Throughout this paranoid era, even peaceful reformers risked arrest: 'liberty', 'democracy' and 'equality' were deemed code-words for revolution.

This book also tells the true stories of the real conspirators against the government, and the tragedies that befell ordinary folk entrapped by *agents provocateurs*. Sometimes this game of cat-and-mouse between the government and its prey descended into high farce. But the stakes were incredibly high: men risked transportation if found guilty of fomenting sedition. And those found guilty of high treason, like Jeremiah Brandreth, suffered an agonizing death on the scaffold...

Chapter One

Enemies of the State

'**I** run great risk of Assassination but I am determined to go through with it and report everything.' This secret agent was terrified that this message to his superiors would be his last. He had infiltrated a republican group planning to attend a huge rally for parliamentary reform at Spa Fields. Now, he was reporting that French-inspired tricoloured uniforms were being made for the big day: 'I expect to be measured for Cloathes [sic] tomorrow and I must go to the Meeting and I expect Arms will be put into my hands.' The spy was worried that he risked arrest whilst performing his mission: 'I shall get away if I can but if I should be taken I expect to be protected.'[1] Fortunately the rally passed off peacefully.

The Machinery of Government

The employment of spies like this anonymous agent was a traditional – indeed an essential – tool of national and local government. On one occasion in 1817, when the alleged misdeeds of one particular spy caused a national scandal, the Prime Minister, Lord Liverpool, declared that 'Spies and informers had been at all times employed by all governments, and ever must be.' The danger was, he said, that occasionally it 'must sometimes happen' that spies overstepped the mark 'from zeal in their business'.[2]

In an age before cameras, telephones, internet or electronic forms of surveillance, sending in a spy was the best way to discover a suspect group's real intentions first-hand. An undercover agent could help nip a conspiracy in the bud before it came to fruition. Spy or informer evidence could be used in court against an alleged or potential offender, even if incriminating papers or letters were hidden or destroyed.

But the idea of state-employed spies and informers affronted the British sense of fair play. Spying on one's friends and neighbours was something the *French* did – it was thoroughly un-English. The French Directory (revolutionary government) was notorious for its use of secret police, spies and informers, whose evidence had sent thousands of men and women to the guillotine. The Radical author William Hone echoed many people's feelings when he declared, 'A spy in social life is a vile imposter, a base and detestable traitor. He works his way by cunning and dissimulation. His manners are artificial, and his conversation false. He is a hypocrite, whose business is to cheat you into a good opinion of him. There is no mixture of good in his character.'[3]

However, until the 1790s British espionage was undertaken on a more or less ad hoc basis. The government's intelligence-gathering was hampered by a lack of permanent resources. Even two decades later, when Alexander Richmond was recruited to spy on the Glasgow weavers, he was surprised to find that the authorities had few reliable men at their disposal: 'Like many others, I imagined they had always at hand a number of experienced agents, ready for any exigency.'[4]

In order to understand how the spy system worked, we must briefly discuss how the machinery of government functioned. Although official government departments dealing with domestic and foreign affairs had existed for several centuries, in 1782 the Home Department (Home Office) and the Foreign Department (Foreign Office) were established in a form roughly corresponding to their modern incarnations. George III had two principal secretaries, or Secretaries of State, in charge of government affairs: one for the Home Department, and one for the Foreign Department. The Home Secretary (as we would call him today) had overall responsibility for maintaining law and order. Henry Dundas was Home Secretary in the early 1790s, followed by the 3rd Duke of Portland, who served under Prime Minister Pitt the Younger.

Initially, the Home Department's staff consisted of: 'The principal secretary, Two under secretaries [sic], Eleven clerks, Two chamber keepers' and 'One necessary woman' (maid or housekeeper). The Home Department also had an under-secretary, along with three clerks dealing with 'plantation affairs' (the British colonies).[5]

When France declared war on Britain in 1793, the authorities realized that this presented a golden opportunity for home-grown revolutionaries.

An armed insurrection was far more likely to succeed if supported by a French invasion. As fears grew over the threat to national security from enemies of the state at home and abroad, the British government adopted a more professional, centralized approach to intelligence-gathering. The Home Office initially took charge of matters relating to the war effort. The following year, a War Department was founded and an additional Secretary of State appointed. The War Department later took over the Home Office's responsibility for the colonies.

In 1793 the Home Office also set up a brand new department. The Alien Office kept watch on foreign visitors (especially suspected French spies) to Britain, and deported them when necessary for national security. Formerly, secret service work was undertaken when needed by an obscure body known as the Foreign Letter Office. The Alien Office appears to have taken over this function at home, although some officials also undertook secret missions in trouble-spots abroad. Under the leadership of the redoubtable William Wickham and Charles William Flint, the Alien Office became the unofficial headquarters of the secret service and a central clearing house for intelligence on foreigners. It had its own premises near the prime minister's official residence in Downing Street, and its officials were primarily Oxford graduates. By 1816 the under-secretary of state at the Home Office had taken over the Alien Office's duties. Unfortunately, a significant quantity of Alien Office records have disappeared, making it difficult to uncover many of its activities.

It was quite common for government officials to move from one department to another. Flint, who became Superintendent of Aliens in 1798, had formerly worked for the Foreign Secretary, while William Wickham was under-secretary at the Home Office from 1798 until early 1801.

The war increased the Home Office's workload and it soon needed extra staff. More clerks were installed, including a 'precis writer' who prepared a brief abstract of all important despatches sent or received by the department, and entered them into a book for the clerks to consult when required. The department also had a 'register of felons in Newgate' (registrar), and even an Arabic interpreter. The Home and Foreign Offices also shared thirty messengers (originally sixteen), a German translator, a secretary of the Latin language, and two 'decipherers'.[6] The 'decipherers' or decoders had a very important task. Since the early eighteenth century, Secretaries of State had had powers to issue warrants to post-masters and post-office clerks to intercept, open and decipher the letters of suspect personages. In Ireland, the Lord Lieutenant could issue warrants to detain the mail.

The Home Secretary also supervised the Transport Service, founded in 1794. The care of prisoners of war was one of its responsibilities, but it also referred letters deemed of interest to the Home Secretary. For example, on 3 March 1812, the Home Secretary wrote to the Post-Masters General (heads of the post-office): 'To desire & hereby authorise you to detain & open all Letters addressed to…Vital a Taylor [sic] residing at No 56 Rupert Street Leicester Fields – & to forward them for inspection of the Commissioners of the Transport Service – and for so doing this shall be your sufficient Warrant.'[7]

Precise records of the number of warrants issued by the Home Office for opening mail were not kept until 1806 (and some were burnt on receipt by post-masters, in order to prevent them getting into the wrong hands). Under normal circumstances only a couple of warrants were issued annually. However, the number increased rapidly in times of great social unrest, such as 1812, the year of the main Luddite outrages, when twenty-eight warrants were issued. A warrant did not necessarily relate to intercepting just one person's mail; several individuals could be named as persons of interest. A warrant could also be issued for all letters potentially relating to a particular offence, such as treason or sedition, which gave the authorities great scope for surveillance. Foreign correspondence could be intercepted, too.

Reformers and rebels knew that their mail was likely to be opened, so they went to great lengths to circumvent the authorities. Assuming an alias was an obvious trick, and sometimes letters were written in code. It's clear from many confidential reports that messages between groups were conveyed face-to-face and letters sent by trusted couriers.

Shortly before the Irish rebellion of 1798, a Chester gentleman was accosted by a dissident Irishman who mistook him for rebel leader Lord Edward Fitzgerald. The loyal Chester man did not enlighten him as to his mistake, and pumped him for information. The Irishman told him that three French invasions were expected, and pikes were being made all around the Dublin area. The Irishman also offered to take his supposed countryman's letters with him to Ireland. When asked how this could be done secretly, the Irishman showed him a special shoe: 'The outer sole of the shoe was open, and a cavity within, so as to contain a letter; which letter he could have covered with strong paper, and have the shoe sewed up, and the letter brought safe.'[8]

The King's Peace

The government's worries were exacerbated by the knowledge that it could not count wholeheartedly on the support of the armed forces. As we shall see later, Royal Navy crews at Spithead and the Nore mutinied in the spring of 1797 over pay and conditions, and many sailors were hanged in consequence. At this time the army was the chief means of quelling disturbances, as Britain had no professional police force until the late 1820s. The King's peace was maintained by an archaic system groaning under the strain of an ever-growing population, and local authorities struggled to cope when serious unrest broke out. Yet many English people felt that a permanent police force would crush traditional civil liberties.

Even the City of London authorities had few resources available for keeping order. By the 1790s, the mighty metropolis was: 'The general receptacle for the idle and depraved of almost every Country, and certainly from every quarter of the dominions of the Crown…the temptations and resources from Criminal Pleasures – Gambling – Fraud and Depredation, as well as for Pursuits of honest industry, almost exceed imagination; since besides being the seat of Government, and the centre of Fashion, Amusements, Dissipation, Extravagance, and Folly, it is not only the greatest commercial City in the Universe, but…[also] one of the first manufacturing Towns.'[9] By 1801, the population of London and Middlesex had reached 845,400 souls, and was still growing.[10]

According to a hardened London magistrate, during the 1790s the capital was home to around 115,000 people living off criminal, illegal or immoral earnings. Citizens were protected by a single watchman or 'Charley' in each parish, who patrolled the London streets at night. These night-watchmen were mostly too old and decrepit to cope with any major outbreaks of violence. Criminals and lawbreakers were kept in check by a relatively small number of policemen linked to the London magistrates' offices.

Before this decade magistrates in the metropolis were unpaid, although they charged fees for certain services such as settling disputes. This caused problems with corruption. In response, the Middlesex Justices Act (1792) increased the number of magistrates' offices to eight (including Bow Street). Each office now had three stipendiary magistrates, and six constables, and, most importantly, they were now all paid by the state. In 1811 the number of constables was doubled, too. The lord chancellor chose the stipendiary magistrates. As they were government appointees, these magistrates were often asked by the Home Office to take charge of special investigations into major security incidents, or to gather intelligence on suspect activities.

Sir William Addington was chief magistrate at Bow Street from 1780 until 1800, followed by Sir Richard Ford. In practice, however, it was Ford who played a leading role in the government's suppression of Radical and seditious societies, including coordinating secret intelligence on their membership and aims, from the mid-1790s until his death in 1806. Ford had a desk in the Home Department and worked closely with the home secretary.

The famed 'Bow Street Runners' were attached to the magistrates' office and court-room at No. 4 Bow St, in Covent Garden. These peace officers (police) knew all the 'flash cribs', 'shades' and 'infernals' where the criminal classes lived.[11] The Runners were sometimes asked to perform investigations in the provinces, and the magistrates also undertook occasional covert missions outside London. The word 'detective' had not yet been coined, but the Runners' duties included gathering information on trouble-makers and infiltrating criminal gangs, sometimes in disguise. The Runners were nicknamed 'Robin Redbreasts' because of their scarlet waistcoats; they went about their duties armed with a cutlass, pistols and truncheon.

After 1805 the roads and lonely heaths around the capital were guarded by the 'Bow Street horse patrole'.[12] These parties of mounted patrols were armed to the teeth and proved highly effective in reducing the numbers of highwaymen who had formerly terrorized travellers. Each officer sported a blue coat with yellow buttons, yellow trousers, and scarlet waistcoat.

The Runners were spurred on to catch criminals by the system of monetary rewards ('blood-money') in place. Anyone who apprehended or aided the arrest of a criminal was entitled to a share of a £40 reward – a considerable sum of money at the time, and worth roughly £4,500 at today's prices. A person who damaged a turnpike 'weighed' (officers' slang for 'was worth') up to £400. Anyone who apprehended a burglar, shoplifter or horse-thief was entitled to a 'Tyburn ticket' granting them exemption from having to undertake parish office (a most unpopular civic duty, because it was unpaid). Tyburn tickets changed hands for twenty to twenty-five guineas in some parishes, so some Bow Street Runners sold these for a nice profit. Even though the Runners and police constables only received a portion of the reward money (perhaps three or four pounds) in each case, because of this they were known to the criminal fraternity as 'blood-hounds', 'thief-takers', or the 'bloody traps'.[13] Spies and informers whose testimony helped bring criminals to justice were also entitled to a share of any reward.

The rewards system led to abuses: 'For the sake of the statutory reward… dark plots have been laid, and men actually seduced into guilt by those who should, by their office, be the ministers of justice.'[14] In 1816 several Bow Street police officers, including Vaughan, Brock, Pelham, and Power, were found to have instigated raw country lads to commit burglaries, in order to later claim the reward money for their capture. Four youths narrowly escaped being hanged following their attempt to break into a house, egged on by Vaughan. In another case, three poor, illiterate Irish labourers were given a job – polishing some round pieces of copper. While busy carrying out this task, they were arrested and charged with imitating the coin of the realm – a crime which then carried the death sentence. Fortunately, someone recognized the police officer who had hired the men. The enterprising police officers involved in both cases were sentenced to death for commissioning these crimes, but later pardoned on a legal technicality.

In the provinces, justice was dispensed by local magistrates (i.e., justices of the peace). A magistrate was often the resident lord of the manor but increasingly, magistrates were affluent members from the ranks of the 'middling-sort'. Except for London and Ireland – where stipendiary magistrates were introduced in the late eighteenth century – justices were usually unpaid volunteers, performing their role as a matter of civic pride.

Magistrates met at the quarter sessions to deal with petty crimes; they were responsible for keeping the peace. They could issue warrants and read the Riot Act when necessary, (i.e. order a disorderly public meeting to disperse). Local magistrates were aided by parish constables or 'peace officers', who were householders serving as part of their civic duty. However, a householder who did not want to serve could pay a deputy to take his place. Constables did not receive a salary, but they could claim for certain expenses, such as travel costs incurred when policing a public execution.

If the magistrates believed that they needed reinforcements, they could call upon the services of large numbers of unpaid special constables to maintain order. These constables were sworn in each year to help preserve the peace in an emergency. For example, in the burgeoning cotton town of Manchester, civil government comprised a borough-reeve (chief official), elected yearly by the inhabitants of the court-leet (criminal court) of the lord of the manor. The borough-reeve was aided by two constables and a deputy constable, who had several beadles (once popularly known as 'bang-beggars!'[15]) under his command. But by 1811, the township of Manchester had about 79,500 inhabitants, so the constables were somewhat out-numbered. Two years later, a stipendiary magistrate was attached to the New Bailey courthouse at Salford, to help cope with the increasing number of cases.

Whenever serious violence was feared, magistrates requested troops from the militia and volunteer yeomanry cavalry to act 'in aid of the civil power'. Each county provided a set number of men to serve in the local militia for five-year terms. The parish constable compiled a muster list of every man between the ages of eighteen to forty-five in his parish, which was sent to the lord-lieutenant of the county. The names of the men who had to serve in the militia were chosen by ballot. Militia service was compulsory, so it was very unpopular, even though the men received a small wage, and a bounty when they joined. The wealthy could pay a substitute to serve in their stead.

The militia provided a trained home reserve force in times of national peril. These soldiers were not normally expected to serve overseas, although some were sent to Ireland in 1798 to quell the insurrection there. Militia-men often had great sympathy with the people they were ordered to police – who often consisted of their own neighbours and families. Therefore, occasionally militia regiments from outside the county were drafted in, if local magistrates doubted the reliability of their own force.

When a foreign invasion was anticipated – as was the case several times during the French revolutionary wars – the government ordered additional or 'supplementary' militia men to be enrolled. Enthusiastic recruits from the more affluent classes rushed to form volunteer regiments and yeomanry cavalry ('horse-soldiers'), such as the Cheshire Yeomanry or the Royal Lancashire Volunteers. These soldiers were expected to furnish their own uniforms and equipment if possible (a yeomanry cavalryman needed a horse), so they needed some private means. Volunteering was very popular, because soldiers who attended drill practice regularly were exempt from militia service. Some volunteer troops grew out of the loyalist associations formed in the backlash against the Radical societies.

In the event, volunteers and yeomanry were far likelier to be called on to aid local justices during local unrest such as food riots and Luddite disturbances, rather than face a foreign invader. These supplementary militia and volunteer regiments were disbanded when peace came.

In dire situations, justices of the peace could request assistance from the regular army to keep order. However, if no troops were available locally, magistrates had to write to the Home Secretary (or the district army commander) to warn that trouble was expected and ask for soldiers. Obviously, it was a far better use of resources to nip potential trouble in the bud, and ensure that troops were already in place before they were needed. Yet, in order to do this, the Home Office needed good, reliable intelligence – and this is why spies were necessary.

Gathering Intelligence

In order to identify and locate persons of interest, Whitehall relied heavily on reports from local magistrates and private gentlemen for news of potential troublemakers in the provinces. Letters poured into the Home Office on a daily basis, and the clerks had the unenviable task of determining which letters and spy reports were important and required immediate action, and which were trivial. Many local justices seem to have been particularly pusillanimous and wrote to Whitehall about every minor happenstance. However, in some areas the justices took a more laid-back approach to correspondence; in 1793 the Home Office only discovered that rioting had taken place in Bristol several days after trouble broke out.

Several local officials employed spies and informers to gather information, which they then forwarded to London. Magistrates like Colonel Ralph Fletcher in Bolton, Reverend William R. Hay in Manchester, and clerk of the peace John Lloyd of Stockport, were very active in this area. Their spies and informers were given code names in correspondence, such as 'B' or 'S', and for extra security, intelligence reports were sent with no name, just the date and location.

The espionage or 'missionary system' was a significant expense for the government. When the Home Office Under-Secretary John Beckett declared his expenses for acquiring intelligence on 27 November 1818, they were £7,161, 3s 11d.[16] These expenses included paying spies directly employed by the Home Office, and reimbursing the Bow Street magistrates and local magistrates for the payments they had made to their own spies. The Home Office was quick to voice concern if local justices overspent. In November 1812, following the Luddite disturbances, Beckett agreed to pay Bolton magistrate Ralph Fletcher's bill of £159 3s 9d for his extensive spy network.[17] A year later, when things had calmed down, Beckett wrote again to say, 'Lord Sidmouth begs that you will reduce the Expense of the Missionary System you have conducted so much to his satisfaction in the way you may think best.'[18]

John Lloyd of Stockport was another diligent intelligence-gatherer. In May 1813 Beckett wrote asking Lloyd to send one of his spies, Michael Hall, to London to receive fresh employment from the Home Secretary, Lord Sidmouth. He also dropped a heavy hint about his expenditure: 'You will be good enough to advance him [Hall] money enough to bear his expenses to London which will also be allowed in your account, together with various small Sums alluded to in your Letter altho' [sic] some of them may have been rather improvidently advanced by you & without authority.'[19]

The flow of information worked both ways. If the Home Office received intelligence that it deemed sufficiently well-founded, it would contact local authorities to ask for help. During the summer of 1812, Under-Secretary Beckett wrote to John Lloyd:

'I have every reason to believe the <u>Blue Anchor</u> at Stockport is a House of extremely bad character…you will immediately make it your Business to ascertain who and what the Persons are that frequent it…what appears to be their object…and what are their real or assumed names – I must at the same time impress upon you the absolute necessity of proceeding with all possible caution in this Inquiry.'

Beckett warned Lloyd that 'Several Persons will arrive at Stockport, about the time when this letter reaches you', and asked to be informed whether or not they appeared. He again stressed the need for secrecy: 'If any suspicion is created you may defeat a plan which I have some reason to think is in agitation.'[20] He promised to send Lloyd more details about the mysterious affair later.

Recruitment

What kind of person was the Home Office, or local magistrates, looking for when they recruited a spy? Lawyers and attorneys were often pressed into service, as they were intelligent and highly literate, and had a clear understanding of the type of evidence that would stand up in court. Military personnel made useful spies, too. Army and navy officers and militia men were asked, or volunteered, to infiltrate the meetings of Radicals, workers' societies and revolutionary groups.

Some spies were patriotic volunteers who genuinely wanted to serve their country, while others were just in it for the money. The remainder were the flotsam and jetsam of the prisons – debtors or criminals who had offered their services to get out of jail. In addition, common informers, often anonymous, would send information against their neighbours or associates to Whitehall or their local justices. Their evidence was highly suspect; they could be working out a grudge or grievance, or hoping for some kind of reward.

Spies were almost always men. If any women were present at the clubs and committees which they infiltrated, they were seemingly invisible, because females are rarely mentioned in the spies' reports. (Although women began to vote at Radical political meetings and to form their own political unions in Lancashire from about 1819.) Women were more likely to act as informants, although a 'Mary Brown' is listed in a 'Key to Agents' Names in Hampden Clubs' in 1817.[21] Pub landladies who rented rooms to Radical groups sometimes had useful information to offer the authorities, as they could often overhear the members' conversations.

Whenever possible, the authorities used local men as spies in areas of unrest, not only because they already knew if these individuals were trustworthy, but also because any stranger asking questions would stick out like a sore thumb – they were bound to be suspected by the groups they were trying to infiltrate. In 1817 Home Secretary Lord Sidmouth wrote to the Lord Advocate of Scotland: 'I know from Experience the extreme, and almost hopeless Difficulty of finding Persons deserving the confidence of their Employers who are capable of acquiring that of the Disaffected belonging to associations in Places where they themselves are Strangers.'[22]

New Ideas

Who were 'the disaffected'? Throughout this era, the upper classes were extremely worried that the lower classes would be led astray by newfangled ideas of equality and democracy, like universal manhood suffrage. The Houses of Parliament represented an exclusive club of noblemen and great landowners with farming, manufacturing and mining interests. The majority of the ruling classes felt that property-holding was the best foundation for wise government. They were accustomed to rule; their sons would inherit the earth; and they felt that the common people enjoyed the blessings of a long-established constitution and religion. The propertied elite greatly resented any suggestion that the uneducated lower orders should have any say in their own government.

During this time period, parliament was dominated by the conservative Tory party, apart from the short-lived Whig 'Ministry of all the Talents' in 1806–1807. In 1783 William Pitt the Younger (1759–1806) took office with George III's backing following the Whig leader Lord Rockingham's death, and the fall of the Shelburne administration. The Whigs (liberals), now led by the 3rd Duke of Portland, became divided in their loyalties because of the war with France. The party split in two when the Duke of Portland and other prominent Whigs joined Pitt's Tory government.

Pitt had become an implacable opponent of parliamentary reform as revolution threatened Britain. Charles James Fox, a supporter of republican ideals, became Pitt's main opponent in the House of Commons, but his extreme views meant that he only had a small band of followers. Pitt virtually had a free hand when his government cracked down on the reformers.

The Tory government kept close watch on the democrats, who were nick-named 'Jacobins' (French revolutionaries) and viewed as 'enemies to all law and order'. The democrats in their turn complained that they were viewed as 'horrid, blood-thirsty wretches who would cut the throat of every man who opposed their vile principles'.[23] In fact, most democrats and reformers, or Radicals as they became known, merely wanted parliamentary reform by peaceful means. Various measures for reform had been mooted for many years, but it had proved impossible to make headway against the upper classes' vested interests.

The electoral system was a slithering mass of corruption: parliamentary seats were bought and sold; the openly unashamed bribery of voters was commonplace; and working-class people had no vote. Large industrial towns like Manchester, Birmingham and Huddersfield had no members of parliament of their own, while 'rotten boroughs' with few inhabitants, such as Old Sarum in Wiltshire, had two. The system was long overdue for reform. The Radicals, who included some prominent Whigs like Charles James Fox, wanted the abolition of rotten boroughs, the introduction of annual parliaments, and a more representative franchise. They harked back to the Magna Carta, the Bill of Rights and the Glorious Constitution of 1688, which they believed had enshrined men's civil liberties and rights. They looked back to a long-lost Saxon golden age in which all men had the vote. (There was unfortunately no historical precedent for universal suffrage.)

The French Revolution opened minds to fresh ideas, to the possibility of a new era of equality, liberty and brotherhood. Writers like Mary Wollstonecraft even advocated the cause of women's rights – a daring notion indeed. The recent American War of Independence too, had not only freed the infant nation from British rule, but also demonstrated that a new system of government was not an idle dream. Subsequently, in Britain there was a great flowering of revolution and constitutional societies dedicated to freedom of speech and thought, trial by jury and a free press.

One of the earliest constitutional societies was founded by Major John Cartwright (1740–1824). He was convinced that 'many of the political evils of the day' emanated from 'ignorance of the principles of the constitution'. This former naval officer, a neat, upright gentleman, had served with distinction until the American War of Independence, but resigned in disgust over what he perceived as Britain's unjust treatment of the colonists. He later served in the Nottingham militia, only to lose his position over political differences with the Lord Lieutenant of the county. Cartwright was also a prolific writer and campaigner for radical reform, who believed that petitioning parliament was the only way forward. The Major was a founder member of the Society of Constitutional Information in 1780, along with John Horne Tooke and others. Even Pitt the Younger, then the great white hope of the reform movement, was a member – ironic considering his later treatment of the Radicals.[24]

The war between old ideas and the new was fought in books, newspapers, magazines and pamphlets. The writings of Thomas Paine (1737–1809) were truly revolutionary. Paine's first great work, *Common Sense* (1776), was a plea for American independence. His second work, *Rights of Man* (1791), was a riposte to Edmund Burke's *Reflections on the Revolution in France* (1790), a powerful attack on French revolutionary ideals, and a plea for maintaining the current status quo.

But it was the second part of Paine's *Rights of Man* (1792) that arguably had the largest influence on Radical thinking. In this book he attacked the institution of monarchy: 'Man has no power over posterity in matters of personal right; and therefore no man, or body of men, had, or can have, a right to set up hereditary government...we cannot conceive a more ridiculous figure of government, than hereditary succession.'[25] He advocated the abolition of the Poor Laws, arguing that the state should provide for the poor, the very young and the elderly. To add fuel to the flames, Paine's *Age of Reason* (1794–5) pilloried organized religion. The ruling elite were appalled by Paine's works, which they viewed as treasonous, seditious and blasphemous.

Paine's pioneering ideas spread like wildfire and were eagerly adopted by the Society of Constitutional Information (which he subsequently joined), and by other so-called 'corresponding societies'. These societies wrote to one another about new Radical ideas, especially parliamentary reform, and disseminated them widely in Britain. One group, the United Englishmen, expressed the views of many freethinkers of the 1790s in its 'Declaration, Resolutions and Constitution':

> *'The House of Commons...is now thoroughly corrupted, and from being the representative of a great and free People, is become a junto of Placemen, Pensioners and Court Dependents...The only effectual remedy...is a* <u>*radical Reform*</u> *of the Representation of the People in Parliament.'*[26]

The London Corresponding Society (LCS), formed in early 1792, advocated universal male suffrage and annual parliaments. (Female suffrage was as yet undreamed-of in most reformers' philosophy, except for a few extremists like Thomas Spence.) The LCS's membership subscription of a penny per week, plus a shilling entrance fee, was affordable even for working-class men. The shoemaker Thomas Hardy and John 'Citizen' Thelwall, a writer and speaker, were some of its most influential members.

Another important group was the Sheffield Society for Constitutional Information (SSCI), which boasted 'nearly two thousand members' and gained new recruits every day. The SSCI 'Resolutions' declared that: 'We have derived more true knowledge from the two works of Mr Thomas Paine, entitled Rights of Man...than from any other author on the subject.' The SSCI unanimously resolved that thanks should be given to Paine 'for the affectionate concern he has shown in his second work on Behalf of the Poor, the Infant and the Aged; who notwithstanding the opulence which blesses other parts of the community, are by the grievous weight of Taxes, rendered the miserable victims of Poverty and wretchedness.'[27]

The SSCI also published a 'declaration', which each new member took when joining: 'I Solemnly declare myself an Enemy to all Conspiracies, Tumults and Riotous proceedings, or maliciously furnishing any attempt that tends to overturn, or any wise Injure or disturb the Peace of the People; or the Laws of this Realm: And that my only wish and design is...praying for a Speedy Reformation, and an Equal Representation in the House of Commons.'[28]

The corresponding societies flourished within the manufacturing districts, and there were similar societies at Manchester (led by Thomas Walker), as well as Leeds, Nottingham and Norwich. However, very few ordinary people joined societies like these, and within such groups, only a tiny minority were dedicated to forcing change through physical force. But the government tarred all reformers with the same brush – and to contemporary eyes, the very idea of letting the people choose their own government was revolutionary in itself and must be suppressed.

The authorities believed they had found evidence of a sinister plot when the LCS wrote to societies like 'the Friends of the Constitution at Paris, known by the name of Jacobins'[29] (that is, French revolutionaries). They sent spies such as 'Citizen Groves' to infiltrate the LCS meetings held at Thelwall's lecture-room in Beaufort's Buildings, the Strand, London.

Even a tiny number of dedicated revolutionaries, if undiscovered, could raise many recruits for their cause, as the United Irishmen would shortly prove. Not all LCS members were committed to reform by peaceful means, according to John Binns, who was also a member of the United Irishmen (see chapter 2). He later wrote that, 'The wishes and hopes of many of its influential members' went beyond its seemingly innocuous objectives 'to the overthrow of the monarch and the establishment of a republic.'[30] Many contemporary observers also believed that: 'Though the ostensible object of this union [the LCS] was a correction of alleged abuses in the representative system, little doubt could be entertained that its real aim was the establishment of a republican form of government upon a similar plan to that of France.'[31]

Treason and Sedition

Following a suggestion by Thomas Paine, the corresponding societies decided to hold a Convention at Edinburgh in late 1792 to discuss parliamentary reform. This was like a red rag (or cap of liberty) to a bullish government. The term 'Convention' smacked not only of republicanism, but also an alternative parliament. The authorities acted swiftly: several delegates were arrested and the Convention dispersed.

The Scottish judiciary, a corrupt arm of the British government, had no difficulty coaxing a packed jury to find two members of Scottish democratic societies, who had attended the Convention, guilty of sedition. Thomas Muir and Thomas Palmer, a lawyer and a clergyman respectively, were transported to Botany Bay. Muir was exiled for fourteen years and Palmer for seven. These were incredibly severe sentences for attending a political meeting, as transportation was normally used for offences like theft or housebreaking.

The reform movement in England was aghast that Muir and Palmer had been treated with such severity, despite the paucity of evidence against them. Then, as news of the horrors unfolding in France reached Britain, reformers found themselves facing a widespread public backlash. On 24 January 1793, Louis XVI died on the guillotine, followed soon after by his wife Marie Antoinette. News of the September 1793 massacres in Paris further strengthened popular feeling against the 'Jacobins' and corresponding societies. Effigies of Tom Paine were burnt in several towns and loyalist associations, or 'Church and King' clubs, formed to counter the democrats. Even pubs put up boards with the inscription 'NO JACOBINS ADMITTED HERE.'[32]

Nothing daunted, the corresponding societies decided to hold another grand meeting: the 'British Convention of the Delegates of the People, associated to obtain Universal Suffrage, and Annual Parliaments'[33] at Edinburgh in late October 1793. Maurice Margarot, William Skirving and Joseph Gerrald were chosen as delegates for the LCS, and the Sheffield society sent Matthew Campbell Browne, editor of the *Patriot* newspaper. On 28 November Margarot, Skirving, Gerrald and others were arrested, and the Convention was broken up.

The result was a foregone conclusion. The following January, Margarot and Skirving were both tried for sedition, found guilty and transported for fourteen years, even though the court witnesses testified that the speeches given at the Convention had promoted reform by peaceful means. Joseph Gerrald, who was tried a few weeks later, was also transported for fourteen years despite an impassioned defence of his liberties in court. Conditions in Australia were far from healthy, and Skirving and Gerrald both died shortly after their arrival.

Soon after, a former spy's plot further boosted the government's war against the Radicals. On 17 May 1794, wine merchant Robert Watt, goldsmith David Downie, Robert Orrock and others were arrested at Edinburgh. Watt and Downie, who had both attended the British Convention the previous year, were charged with high treason. Watt, however, was a former government spy, paid by Home Secretary Henry Dundas to infiltrate a society called the Friends of the People. After a dispute over payment for his services, Watt had switched his allegiance to the rebel cause.

The prosecution alleged that Watt had ordered 4,000 pikes to be made for an insurrection. The men planned to start a fire near the Excise Office in Edinburgh, then take the castle while its garrison tried to extinguish the flames. In his defence, Watt claimed that he had been drawn into the plot 'merely that he might inform government what was going on'.[34] Nevertheless, Watt was found guilty and executed at Edinburgh on 15 October 1794, while his accomplice Downie was convicted but spared execution.

When the LCS held a mass meeting at Chalk Farm in April 1794, the audience was crawling with government spies, including special agent James Walsh (whom we shall meet again later). Walsh was not very well disguised; he wore a 'King and Constitution' badge (to show his loyalty to the monarchy), and he was outed as 'a spy from the Treasury' by a fellow spy, Citizen Groves.[35]

Meanwhile, the government had received information of Irish support for a French invasion. Its spies had also discovered that the LCS planned another Convention. The government put two and two together; it knew that there were links between the Irish and British democrats, and the LCS had links with France. But the backing of parliament was required before taking its next step – the suspension of Habeas Corpus – the constitutional safeguard against arbitrary imprisonment without trial.

Before the Convention could meet, on 12 September 1794 LCS members John Thelwall, Thomas Hardy and others were arrested (and some of the SSCI democrats), and all their papers confiscated. Another Radical, the writer and printer John Horne Tooke, was arrested after one of his letters was intercepted by the Home Office. A House of Commons select committee was set up to examine these papers, and it was given the government's spy reports so that it could consider all this evidence. The Committee reported that the proposed Convention 'must be considered as a Traitorous Conspiracy for the subversion of the established Laws and Constitution, and the Institution of that fatal system of Anarchy and confusion which has fatally prevailed in France.'[36]

Parliament was now convinced of the need for drastic measures, and the Habeas Corpus Act was suspended, despite Whig protests. This meant that any person could be arrested without a trial. The major newspapers swung behind the government and supported this action. The government quickly arrested more members of the corresponding societies in London, Sheffield and Norwich. After being examined by the privy council, Horne Tooke, Hardy and Thelwall were charged with high treason: plotting to kill the King. While Hardy was in prison his pregnant wife, terrified that her husband would be hanged, lost her baby and died soon afterwards.

The Radicals' trials took place at the Old Bailey that autumn, shortly after Robert Watt died on the scaffold at Edinburgh. Hardy was tried first and several spies testified against him, including Groves, George Lynam, and George Sanderson. Much of their evidence was pathetically weak, and Hardy's defence counsel, Thomas Erskine, made mincemeat of them.

Embarrassingly for Pitt the Younger, who was now Prime Minister, John Horne Tooke called him as a character witness, to prove that the statesman had formerly been in favour of parliamentary reform. However, 'the spirit and independence of an English jury'[37] saved the Radicals from a fate like that of Muir and Palmer in Scotland. With little evidence of treason against them, Hardy, Tooke and Thelwall were found not guilty, although several members of the LCS languished in prison for some time.

The government's campaign in England had misfired. The triumphant acquittals of the Radicals led to an increase in the popularity of the London Corresponding Society, and it acquired many new members, including the breeches-maker Francis Place (who was later careful to distance himself from any suggestion of illegal activities). By the late spring of 1795, over 2,000 members were attending LCS meetings each week. Its ranks were swelled by public resentment of high food prices, owing to a grain shortage following a dreadful harvest. On 26 October, the London Corresponding Society held a mass protest against the war with France in the fields near Copenhagen House. The meeting was peaceful and orderly, despite the huge numbers in attendance, but a handbill was distributed bearing the treasonous title 'King-killing no Murder'.[38]

Then, three days later on 29 October, when the King went to open parliament, crowds gathered around the state carriage, calling out 'Bread! Bread! Peace! Peace!'[39] A bullet or stone passed through one of the royal carriage windows. When the King returned to the Queen's House, people attempted to stop the coach and drag George III outside, but his guards rescued him.

This so-called assassination attempt (some Radicals believed it was the action of a government agent provocateur) gave Pitt the excuse he needed to crack down on the political and corresponding societies. Two acts of parliament were passed which proscribed all political agitation. The Treasonable Practices Act of 1795 extended the scope of the law on treason, so that 'compassing or imagining the death of the King' by means of any writing or printed matter was now a treasonable offence. The second Act aimed to prevent seditious meetings and assemblies. In effect it outlawed all political meetings, even those merely preparing a petition to parliament, except those held under very strict conditions. A meeting could be broken up by magistrates if any language disrespectful of the government was used, and if twelve or more people attending a meeting were still together an hour after it had been ordered to disperse, they could be deemed felons.

The government's measures were highly effective. Membership of the reform societies plummeted. The new legislation meant that opponents of the government faced jail or transportation if they held meetings. Some factions within the reform societies began to despair of using peaceful means to effect reform, and their thoughts turned to revolution. As the Tories' grip on the nation grew ever tighter, Charles James Fox could do little but make fine speeches as Pitt's government snuffed out the lamps of liberty one by one.

Democracy was now a dirty word, but the government could not afford to rest on its laurels. Now its biggest worry was Ireland, long regarded as Britain's Achilles heel. A French invasion there would be a catastrophe.

Chapter Two

Spies, Ships and Secrets

Ireland's problems had dogged British politics for centuries. Until 1782 the Irish Parliament had been controlled by England. However, the Rockingham administration was forced to grant Irish legislative independence following pressure from the 'Patriots,' headed by Henry Grattan and the Volunteer movement. The Volunteers (primarily Protestants) originated as loyalist associations formed by concerned Belfast citizens in 1779, during fears of a French invasion when the American Revolutionary War was at its height.

In theory, Grattan's new parliament was independent of Westminster. Ireland now had its own parliament, with a House of Lords and House of Commons. Dublin Castle was its administrative centre. But for all practical purposes, Ireland remained subject to English rule and political influence. The holders of key Irish administrative positions, such as the Lord Lieutenant and Lord Chancellor, owed their places to the British prime minister's patronage. The Great Seal of England still ratified each new Irish law.

Ireland suffered from massive economic and political disadvantages, and deep religious divisions. Its people lived in the most abject poverty, which was intensified by trade restrictions designed to protect English textiles, preventing Irish woollen goods from being exported to England or the British colonies. The Irish franchise was concentrated in the hands of the Protestant ruling class or 'ascendancy' which owned virtually all the land. Two-thirds of the seats in the Irish House of Commons were returned by fewer than a hundred voters. Votes were openly bought and sold, and pensions bestowed on the establishment's friends, no matter how infamous their characters. Roman Catholics – the vast majority of the population – were excluded from the Irish parliament; they had no voting rights and could not hold public office. Protestants hogged all the key positions in the army, navy, the law, commissions of the peace, etc.

William Pitt was prepared to grant some relief to the disadvantaged Roman Catholics and to reduce Ireland's unfair trade restrictions. However, he was hamstrung by ultra-Tories in his own party, and by George III's sincerely held belief that granting Catholic emancipation would violate his coronation oath. The 1788 Regency crisis caused by George III's illness (possibly porphyria) caused great tension between the two governments, because Grattan's parliament tried to assert its independence by asking the Prince of Wales to become Regent of Ireland, with unlimited powers.

Pitt's Tories, on the other hand, were desperate to delay a Regency for as long as possible. They thought that the Prince, who had friends among the Foxite Whigs (Fox's supporters), would seize the opportunity to turf out the Tories when he gained power. A Regent in Ireland with unlimited privileges could create as many peers as he liked, and tip the balance of power in parliament. If there was to be a Regency, then the Tories wanted to set strict limits on the Prince's powers. If the Prince refused a Regency on those terms and the Queen was made Regent instead, then the constitutional spectre was raised of two different Regents in two kingdoms.

Luckily for the Tories, the King recovered in early 1789. But this abortive attempt by Ireland to assert its independence strengthened the hand of those, like Pitt, who wanted a Union of the two kingdoms – and made Irish nationalists even more convinced that a complete break from Westminster was necessary.

Growing Tensions

Ireland's problems were magnified by social and religious tensions which regularly erupted into horrific violence. To give just one example, during the 1790s the Protestant and Presbyterian 'Peep-O'-Day Boys' attacked and burned the houses of Catholics in Armagh. To protect themselves, the Catholics formed armed associations known as the 'Defenders'. After a terrific battle between the two factions at Diamond (a cross-roads in Armagh) in September 1795, some Protestants formed the first Orange Lodge with the avowed intention to exterminate all Roman Catholics.

Yet some Irishmen had more liberal views. Theobald Wolfe Tone, Samuel Neilson and others wanted to promote religious toleration, extend the franchise to disadvantaged Catholics, and push for parliamentary reform. Wolfe Tone (1763–1798) recalled that the thunderbolt of the French Revolution, and the ensuing battle between Edmund Burke and Thomas Paine for British hearts and minds, 'changed in an instant the politics of Ireland'. This 'oppressed, plundered, and insulted nation…sympathised most sincerely with the French people, and watched their progress to freedom with the utmost anxiety.'[1]

The Society of United Irishmen of Belfast was founded by Wolfe Tone and others in 1791. Tone, a coach-maker's son, had always longed to be a soldier. He studied mathematics at Trinity College, Dublin, at his father's insistence, but his rebellious nature made his time at university a stormy one. Tone later studied law but soon got caught up in the excitement of revolutionary politics. The Society, which extolled the works of Thomas Paine, called on its fellow countrymen to form more societies to promote knowledge of the constitution, and the 'abolition of bigotry in religion and politics, and the equal distribution of the Rights of Man through all Sects and Denominations of Irishmen'.[2]

A few weeks later, the Society of United Irishmen of Dublin was founded, with James Napper Tandy as Secretary. It too was 'composed of all religious persuasions' and had very similar aims to the Belfast group, such as a fairer representation in parliament, because, it argued, Ireland had no 'National Government'. Ireland's MPs considered themselves 'as the Representatives of their own Money, or the hired servants of the English Government; whose Minister here, is appointed for the sole purpose of dealing out Corruption'. The Society complained that Ireland was kept in a 'state of abject slavery' by the British government.[3]

At this date the United Irishmen's aims were entirely legal, peaceful and constitutional. In 1794 the society declared its support for universal manhood suffrage. Members were primarily drawn from the middle classes, and included Catholics and Protestants (some like Napper Tandy were former Volunteers). They tried to damp down the ongoing feuds and outbreaks of violence between Protestants and Catholics.

In 1793, in an attempt to stave off calls for full emancipation, the Irish parliament agreed to give Roman Catholic freeholders of property (worth forty shillings) the vote. The following year, Pitt appointed Lord Fitzwilliam as Lord Lieutenant of Ireland, but when the King heard that Fitzwilliam was taking steps towards full Catholic emancipation, he put pressure on Pitt. Fitzwilliam was recalled to England within a few weeks of his arrival in Dublin. Following this immense disappointment for the Roman Catholics, the Defenders became more nationalistic in their aims. Many Irishmen believed that a civil war was now inevitable between the Protestant landowners and Catholic peasantry.

As civil war loomed, the government at Dublin passed several laws to deal with potential troublemakers. Local magistrates were given sweeping powers to search for arms and disperse meetings. Militia regiments were embodied; all weapons had to be licensed; public meetings were made illegal, and societies like the United Irishmen made unlawful. Prominent members of the United Irishmen, including Simon Butler and Archibald Hamilton Rowan (who had attended the British Convention – see chapter 1), were tried for seditious libel, fined £500 and sentenced to two years' imprisonment in Dublin's Newgate Gaol.

Unfortunately, the United Irishmen had become bitterly divided. Although their views were not yet shared by a majority in the society, members such as Wolfe Tone and Lord Edward Fitzgerald grew convinced that revolution was the only way to achieve reform in Ireland and throw off the oppression of the Protestant Ascendancy. Tone and Fitzgerald believed that an armed insurrection, perhaps aided by the Catholic Defenders, and with French backing, might just succeed. But another faction, which included Thomas Addis Emmet and Dr William McNevin, did not want assistance from a foreign invader.

A Spy is Caught

Meanwhile, the British and Irish governments needed to keep tabs on potential troublemakers in Ireland. Much money was spent on hiring spies and informers. The authorities found it virtually impossible to plant any spies amongst the close-knit Catholic Defenders, but it proved easier to penetrate the United Irishmen's ranks. A close watch was kept on any Irishmen travelling to revolutionary France, and on any suspected French agents arriving in Britain.

In 1794 an Irishman, Reverend William Jackson, was sent by the French Directory to spy out Ireland's ripeness for invasion. Jackson seems rather naive and clumsy to have been entrusted with such a delicate mission. He stopped in London while en route to Ireland and engaged a lawyer named Cockayne to act as his secretary. Cockayne instantly notified the government of Jackson's mission and he was asked to keep the Irishman under surveillance.

At this point Lawrence McNally enters the picture. This handsome barrister with twinkling eyes was a popular Irish playwright and orator. McNally (or MacNally) was often employed by the United Irishmen as their defence counsel. He introduced Jackson and Cockayne to Hamilton Rowan, the United Irishman still in prison at Dublin. The report Jackson and Cockayne were compiling for the French Directory was, naturally, in French and Rowan offered to correct their French grammar. Cockayne gave Rowan a pen and ink so he could make the necessary adjustments.

The moment Jackson's back was turned, Cockayne took the document, now covered with amendments in Rowan's handwriting, to the Privy Council. This was sufficient evidence for the government to hang Rowan. (The burden of proof was less strict in an Irish court of law than in England; the word of just one witness was sufficient to convict someone of high treason.) Luckily for Rowan, the flow of information travelled both ways. The United Irishmen had their own spies in government quarters. Rowan's wife had a friend on the Privy Council, who warned her about this incriminating document, and she successfully organized a daring escape for her husband.

McNally also arranged a meeting between Jackson and Wolfe Tone. The republican told Jackson that if France invaded England, the whole populace would unite against the foreigners: an invasion of Ireland was a much safer bet. Tone offered to go to France and speak to the Directory about the state of Ireland. But, unnerved by Jackson's lack of caution, he soon withdrew his offer, making sure that Cockayne heard him (to ensure that he could not testify against him). Shortly afterwards, Jackson was arrested in Ireland. Meanwhile, Tone and his fellow United Irishmen sweated, wondering whether Jackson would try to save his skin by betraying them. Pressure was put on Tone to give evidence against Jackson, but he refused. Influential friends interceded with the Irish government on Tone's behalf, and he was allowed to go into voluntary exile in America.

Jackson was charged with treason and conspiring to bring about a revolution, but it took twelve months for him to be brought to trial. As Lawrence McNally was acting as his lawyer, Jackson asked him to witness his will, in which he commended his wife and children to the French nation, and to McNally's care. This public document implicated McNally as a United Irishman, and he turned it over to the government.

It was probably at this point that McNally was recruited to spy for the authorities. His codename in the state correspondence was 'J.W.',[4] and he received a secret government pension for his services. Because 'Mac', as he was known to his friends, was completely trusted by the United Irishmen, they confided all their secrets to him. McNally was able to alert the government to any evidence of use to the state prosecutor.

Although Cockayne was the only witness against Jackson, the clergyman was found guilty. On 30 April 1795, Jackson took poison and expired in court before sentence could be passed.

The following month, Tone and his family left Ireland for America, with secret instructions from the United Irishmen to continue negotiations with France. After less than a year in America, Tone made his way to Paris, which he reached in February 1796. There he was reunited with his brother Matthew, 'a sincere and ardent republican',[5] and later he met up with another United Irishman, Edward John Lewins (or Lewines). Lewins was negotiating to obtain French troops and was also talking to the Spanish and Dutch (then English enemies) regarding naval support for an invasion.

That summer two United Irishmen – Lord Edward Fitzgerald and Arthur O'Connor – met General Louis Lazare Hoche, one of France's most daring revolutionary generals, in Switzerland. They reinforced Tone's pleas that the Irish people were suffering great oppression by their rulers and only French intervention could save them. In June, Fitzgerald and O'Connor signed a treaty with Hoche and the French Directory to provide men, arms and a fleet. But several months passed before Tone's plans finally bore fruit.

The Bantry Bay Disaster

In the middle of December 1796, General Hoche and Wolfe Tone sailed from Brest, France with over 40 vessels and 15,000 troops. If this invasion force had landed safely the history of Ireland might have changed forever. But the French fleet encountered appalling weather, and only 14 ships and about 6,000 men reached Bantry Bay, Ireland, just before Christmas. The frigate containing Hoche and his Admiral was separated from the fleet by the storms, and never arrived.

The fleet remained anchored off the coast for six days, at times less than 500 yards from the shore, 'near enough to toss a biscuit ashore',[6] Tone remembered. The fleet remained unmolested by British ships but was at the mercy of the waves. The shores of Ireland were wide open to the would-be invaders. To Tone's fury, the French commander, Grouchy, just dithered. The troops did not make landfall and no Irishmen rose up to join them.

At this time Britain's home seas were protected by two main fleets: the Channel fleet, based at Spithead and commanded by Lord Bridport, and Admiral Duncan's North Sea squadron. As the wind and weather continued battering the French ships, the invaders grew short of supplies, and increasingly nervous that Bridport's Channel Fleet would appear. Wolfe Tone's ship and the tattered remains of Hoche's fleet turned tail and sailed for France.

The Black Legion Arrives

Although the main event was unsuccessful, a second fleet arrived in Britain a few weeks later. (It's unclear why it didn't take place simultaneously with the Bantry Bay expedition, unless the weather was a factor.) General Hoche had ordered Colonel William Tate, an American veteran of the Revolutionary War, to land at or near Cardigan Bay. Alternatively, if Tate found the mouth of the River Severn undefended, he was to sail up the Severn and burn down Bristol – Britain's second largest port. After razing the port, docks and ships to the ground, Tate would carry on up the coast to Chester and Liverpool.

The expedition included over 1,000 men and was known as the Legion Noire (Black Legion), because the soldiers involved wore dark jackets.

Its three main objectives were: 'if possible, to raise an insurrection in the country';[7] secondly, to disrupt British commerce; and thirdly, to assist another invasion attempt by diverting the defending armed forces. Tate was to incite the poorest people to rebel and rob munitions stores by giving them money and drink, and tell them that the government was the cause of their distress.

On Wednesday 22 February 1797, the small fleet led by Tate was observed near the coast of Ilfracombe in Devon. The French vessels scuttled several merchant ships. The local militia was raised by Colonel Orchard of Bideford, but the enemy ships left the area as Orchard's North Devon Volunteers prepared to march.

The invaders were next spotted from the heights of St Bride's Bay on the Pembrokeshire coast. Two frigates, a corvette, and a lugger were seen steering from the Bristol Channel towards St David's Head. The ships 'showed English colours, but were soon suspected to be French'. After rounding St David's Head, and anchoring briefly off a small promontory, the enemy vessels sailed towards the small but busy port of Fishguard, 'finally anchoring in a small bay, near Lanonda [Llanwnda] church. They immediately hoisted French colours, and put out their boats. The country-people were dreadfully alarmed, and instantly abandoned their houses.'[8]

The French soldiers scaled the cliffs at Carreg Wastad, then set the turf ablaze to let their commander know they were safely ashore. The invaders were barefoot, dressed in rags, and starving. They ransacked the locals' houses, looking for food, and burnt every stick of furniture they could find for warmth. Even feather mattresses were ripped open and the cotton ticking used to make trousers for warmth. Two Welshmen were killed, and a local woman, Mary Williams (also known as Matty Carham), who was heavily pregnant, was mistreated by an ungallant French soldier. The King later granted her a pension of £40 per annum as compensation for her ordeal.[9]

By Thursday evening, the local commander, Lord Cawdor, had arrived with as many volunteer troops as he could muster: his own troop of Yeoman Cavalry from Castlemartin, plus the Pembroke Fencibles, the Fishguard and Newport Fencibles, and part of the Cardiganshire militia – over 600 men in total. The French forces greatly outnumbered the volunteers, but they were in very poor shape; many were former galley slaves, who had been freed if they promised to serve. They quickly surrendered.[10] According to local tradition (possibly apocryphal) one plucky local heroine, Jemima Nicholas, single-handedly captured several Frenchmen while armed only with a pitchfork.

A later account of the French surrender was provided by the writer Richard Ayton, who visited Fishguard in about 1813 and spoke to several local people. They told him that when the French soldiers halted on Goodwich Sands, they spotted the local militia above them on higher ground, almost within musket-shot range. Lord Cawdor's troops were followed by their womenfolk, who feared for their men's safety: 'The women in the rear were all clad, according to the custom of the country, in red woollen shawls... and these, together with their black beaver hats, gave them not only a masculine but also a very martial appearance; the French mistook them for a reserve of troops, and immediately gave up the contest in despair.'[11]

Despite the incursion's failure, British officials suspected that the French must have had local help and a witch-hunt ensued. Several Dissenters were arrested (not being a member of the established church was then viewed as suspicious), and two men were charged with treason. In September 1797 an Anabaptist preacher, Thomas John, and yeoman Samuel Griffiths were tried at the Great Sessions at Haverfordwest.[12]

The prosecution asserted that John and Griffiths had gone into the French camp at Fishguard to pass on intelligence about the local defences and military force, and to assure the commander that the countryside would rally to their cause. In fact, Griffiths had been captured by the Frenchmen, but Colonel Tate released him shortly afterwards. Thomas John had simply wandered over to the invasion site to see what all the excitement was about. The prosecution's evidence relied on statements given by the French prisoners of war, and an American prisoner named Prudhomme. But they refused to testify against the two Welshmen, as they were afraid they would face retribution for helping the British authorities when they returned to France. Both men were acquitted; the evidence against them was flimsy, to say the least, and their arrests were probably motivated by local spite.

News of the French landing electrified the nation, despite the invaders' lack of success. Britons flocked to join volunteer regiments, and patriotic gentlemen were on the alert for any possible dangers from the disaffected.

The government remained watchful, convinced that an invasion was still a clear and present danger.

Following the Bantry Bay fiasco, Tone was still pressing for an invasion of Ireland, this time with a combined force of French and Dutch ships. The French fleet was then at Brest, and the Dutch fleet was at Texel in the Netherlands. The British government had little definitive intelligence of the whereabouts of the two main enemy fleets or their ultimate destinations, but an invasion was still widely expected, and Bridport's Grand Fleet patrolled the Channel in readiness. Then news broke of a full-blown mutiny in the Royal Navy – the nation's pride, and its primary defence.

Mutiny!

Living conditions in the British fleet were dreadful. Ordinary seamen were poorly paid – wages had not increased since Charles II's reign – and their rations were scarcely fit for human consumption. Discipline was strict; officers and men were not allowed to go ashore when their ships were anchored in their home port to prevent desertion. In order to ensure sufficient manpower, merchant seamen were kidnapped by press-gangs when in port and forced to serve in the Royal Navy; some were also forcibly 'pressed' from their ships when war broke out. Each area of Britain provided a set number of men for the navy, and these 'quota-men' received a bounty if they agreed to serve.

Many seamen were poor men who had volunteered purely for the bounty. These cash payments were extremely tempting to debtors and bankrupts, but once their debts were paid off, they had little incentive to work hard. Local magistrates also had the power to send rogues and beggars to serve in the navy as an alternative to prison, so there was a significant criminal element on board many ships. In Ireland, magistrates had used this facility since about 1795, to get rid of troublesome United Irishmen and Catholic Defenders. However, some United Irishmen also served as volunteers so that they could incite trouble in the fleet.

A brutal system of floggings was used to enforce discipline amongst these motley crews; some officers were deemed cruel even by contemporary standards. By late 1796, many lower ranks in the navy had had enough. At first they tried to effect change through peaceful means. In early 1797 seamen from several ships in the Channel fleet sent polite petitions requesting a pay increase to the former commander-in-chief of the Channel fleet, Lord Howe. But, as Howe was unwell and no longer in charge of the fleet, he took no official action. The men were furious that their requests had been ignored and on 16 April, the crews on the ships at Spithead, including the *Queen Charlotte* and *Royal George*, went on strike. They refused to put to sea as ordered until their pay was raised, and red flags of mutiny were run up the flagpoles.

The seamen who mutinied were primarily concerned with improving their pay and conditions, rather than expressing disloyalty to Britain. Great care was taken to maintain discipline amongst the mutineers. They were highly organized. Each ship had its own central committee; another committee comprised two delegates from each disaffected ship. The men also took an oath of allegiance to support one another and their cause.

The mutiny horrified the government – and the nation. The strength of feeling amongst the men was so solid that Lord Bridport, the Channel Fleet commander, had no option but to ask parliament to meet at least some of the mutineers' demands. They were given a substantial pay rise and offered a free pardon for their disobedience. When the mutineers received this news most were extremely pleased and by 23 April the mutiny appeared over. It seemed that the government had averted disaster. Yet trouble arose again when doubts surfaced over whether the promised pay rise would materialize.

On 7 May the men of the *London* at Spithead mutinied afresh and three officers were imprisoned; soon more ships mutinied at St Helens, a harbour on the Isle of Wight. Lord Howe went to speak to the men at St Helens and Spithead in person. Once their grievances were addressed, the seamen returned to their duty. A few days later most of Bridport's ships weighed anchor and made for Brest, to ensure that the French invasion fleet based there could not break out. Just a few disgruntled men o'war remained at Plymouth.

In the meantime, a copycat mutiny broke out on 12 May, this time at the Nore (Sheerness), an anchorage in the Thames estuary. The chief of the Nore delegates was Richard Parker, a well-educated seaman from Exeter, who served on the *Sandwich*. Parker took charge of the men's negotiations with the authorities. The Nore mutineers wanted better wages, like the Spithead men, but they had some additional demands, such as a fairer distribution of the prize-money awarded when an enemy ship was taken.

When news reached the Nore of the terms agreed at Spithead, and the King's pardon, the Admiralty supposed that the men would back down. But the Admiralty refused to grant the extra concessions demanded by the Nore mutineers. The seamen showed their mettle by seizing some gunboats in Sheerness harbour and firing on the local fort. Effigies of William Pitt and Lord Dundas were hanged at the yard-arm – a ghoulish indication of political feelings amongst the mutineers. The language used by many ships' delegates was clearly modelled on Thomas Paine's works, as the men talked of their rights and liberties. The mutinous ships were dubbed the 'Floating Republic'.[13]

Contemporaries believed that the mutineers had been infiltrated by Jacobins. Two members of the London Corresponding Society, Dr Watson and John Bone, went to visit the sailors at Portsmouth and contacted one of the ships at the Nore. The previous year, Wolfe Tone had urged his countrymen in the British fleet to rise up. A United Irishman named Lee was later hanged for his part in the Plymouth mutiny and it seems likely that, as there were many Irish crew-members, some mutineers had their own political agenda.

However, most of the seamen on board the disaffected ships were loyalists who had joined the protests mainly because they wanted better pay and conditions, not to fight their King and country. The Nore mutiny would probably have died down, if left to itself, yet in late May, some ships from Admiral Duncan's fleet (then at Yarmouth) sailed to the Nore and joined the mutiny, instead of going to the Texel to watch the Dutch as ordered.

The authorities retaliated by stopping supplies of food and water to the mutinous ships. All communications between ships and shore were cut off, except between the ringleaders and the Admiralty's agents. The mutineers retaliated by blocking the River Thames with a line of ships to paralyse trade. The rebel ships captured any naval supply ships attempting to slip through the blockade and purloined their foodstuffs. But there was so much traffic in the Thames that the mutineers could not maintain the blockade efficiently, and Parker ordered it to cease. The delegates on the ships now resorted to intimidation to maintain their ascendancy, and several ringleaders discussed trying to escape to France with their ships.

William Pitt strengthened the government's hand against the mutineers with some temporary legislation; anyone who tried to excite mutiny or rebellion in the army or navy, or held a treasonous meeting, would face a death sentence. The general public had initially shown sympathy with the seamen's original demands for better pay and conditions. Now the mutineers' refusal to protect their native shores against the French had turned public opinion firmly against them.

One by one, ships slipped away from the rebel fleet, and surrendered to the authorities. By 14 June the mutiny was a spent force. Richard Parker and over twenty of the ringleaders were hanged. On the Continent meanwhile, Wolfe Tone had heard of the mutinies, and was desperate not to squander this precious opportunity for invasion. Yet, the fleet at Brest was not ready for action and the Texel fleet was hampered by the weather. When the Dutch fleet finally ventured out of the Texel in October, it was trounced by Admiral Duncan at Camperdown. Several of Duncan's ships were former mutineers.

The 'Spy Nozy' Affair

After all this excitement Britain was on high alert. The Home Department at Whitehall took swift action when it received alarming reports about some highly suspicious characters, possibly French, who had been seen wandering about the Quantock Hills, about twenty miles from Bristol – one of the invasion fleet's targets.

On 11 August 1797, Dr Daniel Lysons, a Bath resident, wrote to the Home Office to report his fears about the new tenants at Alfoxton House, near the little village of Holford, Somerset:

'On the 8th inst. I took the liberty to acquaint your Grace with a very suspicious business concerning an emigrant family, who have contrived to get possession of a Mansion House at Alfoxton, late belonging to the Rev. Mr. St. Albyn, under Quantock Hills. I am since informed, that the Master of the House has no wife with him, but only a Woman who passes for his Sister. The man has Camp Stools, which he & his visitors carry with them

when they go about the country upon their nocturnal or diurnal excursions,
& have also a Portfolio in which they enter their observations, which they
have been heard to say were almost finished. They have been heard to say
they should be rewarded for them, & were very attentive to the River near
them - probably the River coming within a mile or two of Alfoxton from
Bridgewater. These people may possibly be under Agents to some principal
at Bristol.'[14]

Dr Lysons need not have feared; the Home Department had already sent someone to investigate. On the very same day that Lysons penned his letter, special agent and Bow Street Runner James Walsh had already made his way to the Bear Inn at Hungerford to conduct initial enquiries. There he interviewed a former servant from Alfoxton, Charles Mogg, and sent his findings to his employer, John King, Under-Secretary of State:

'Sir,
    Charles Mogg says that he was at Alfoxton last Saturday...he there
met Thomas Jones who lives in the Farm House at Alfoxton, who informed
Mogg that some French people had got possession of the Mansion House
and that they were washing and Mending their cloaths all Sunday...That
Christopher Trickie and his Wife who live at the Dog pound at Alfoxton,
told Mogg that the French people had taken the plan of Their House, and
that They had also taken the plan of all the places round that part of the
Country, that a Brook runs in front of Trickie's House and the French
people inquired of Trickie wether [sic] the Brook was Navigable to the Sea,
and upon being informed by Trickie that It was not, They were afterwards
seen examining the Brook quite down to the Sea...Mogg spoke to some other
persons inhabitants of that Neighbourhood, who all told him they thought
these French people very suspicious persons and that They were doing no
good there ... The French people kept no Servant but were visited by a
number of Persons, and were frequently out upon the heights most part of the
night... As Mr. Mogg is by no means the most intelligent Man in the World,
I thought it my Duty to send You the whole of his Story as he related It.'[15]

King replied next day with fresh orders:

'You will immediately proceed to Alfoxton or its neighbourhood yourself, taking care on your arrival so to conduct yourself as to give no cause of suspicion to the Inhabitants of the Mansion house there – you will narrowly watch their proceedings, & observe how they coincide with Mogg's account...You will give me a precise account of all the circumstances you observe...you will of course ascertain the names of the persons, & will add their descriptions – & above all you will be careful not to give them any cause of alarm, that if necessary they should be found on the spot. Should they however move, you must follow their tracks and give me notice thereof, and of the place to which they have betaken themselves. I herewith transmit you a bank note of £20.'[16]

On 15 August Walsh wrote again to King. He was staying at the 'Globe Inn, [Nether] Stowey, Somerset... which although it is five Miles from Alfoxton, is the nearest house I can get any accommodation at'. By now he had discovered that the new tenants were the poet William Wordsworth (1770–1850), and his sister Dorothy.

'I had not been many minutes in this house before I had an opportunity of entering upon my Business, By a Mr. Woodhouse asking the Landlord, If he had seen any of those Rascalls from Alfoxton. To which the Landlord reply'd, He had seen Two of them Yesterday. Upon which Woodhouse asked the Landlord, If <u>Thelwall</u> was gone. I then asked if they meant the famous Thelwall. They said yes. That he had been down some time, and that there were a Nest of them at Alfoxton House who were protected by a Mr. Poole a Tanner of this Town, and that he supposed Thelwall was there (Alfoxton House) at this time. I told Woodhouse that I had heard somebody say at Bridgewater that They were French people at the Manor House. The Landlord and Mr. Woodhouse answered, No. No. They are not French, But they are people that will do as much harm as All the French can do...

I think this will turn out no French affair, but a mischiefuous [sic] gang of disaffected Englishmen. I have just procured the Name of the person who took the House. His name is Wordsworth a name I think known to Mr. Ford [the Bow St magistrate].'[17]

'The famous Thelwall' Walsh mentioned was 'Citizen' John Thelwall, the noted Radical, whom Walsh had been investigating for years. The next day Walsh gave more particulars of Alfoxton's suspicious new tenants:

> *'The inhabitants of Alfoxton House are a Sett of violent Democrats. The House was taken for a Person of the name of Wordsworth, who came to it from a Village near Honiton in Devonshire, about five Weeks since. The Rent of the House is secured to the Landlord by a Mr. Thomas Poole of this Town. Mr. Poole is a Tanner and a Man of some property. He is a most Violent Member of the Corresponding Society and a strenuous supporter of Its Friends. He has with him at this time a Mr. Coldridge* [Coleridge] *and his Wife both of whom he has supported since Christmas last. This Coldridge came last from Bristol and is reckoned a Man of Superior Ability. He is frequently publishing, and I am told is soon to produce a new work. He has a Press in the House and I am informed He prints as well as publishes his own productions.'*[18]

It is not clear exactly how or why Wordsworth's name was already known to the authorities – unless they knew that he had visited France twice. (His biographer Kenneth Johnston has speculated that Wordsworth spied for the secret service abroad). William's first visit was smack in the turmoil of the French Revolution, on the eve of the first Federation Day, 14 July 1790 – the anniversary of the storming of the Bastille.

> *'Bliss was it in that dawn to be alive!*
> *But to be young was very heaven!'*[19]

On Wordsworth's second trip to France he visited the National Assembly, and Jacobin Club, and fell in love with the vivacious Annette Vallon, who became pregnant with his child. William returned to England, hoping to raise funds for their baby, but the lovers were separated by the war with France. William and his sister Dorothy set up home together. In 1795 William met Samuel Taylor Coleridge, and a famous literary friendship blossomed. The Wordsworths moved to Alfoxton (Alfoxden) House, not far from Coleridge's cottage at Nether Stowey, and the two men, accompanied by Dorothy, went on long walks together over hill and dale. When the Wordsworths were spotted examining the nearby river, they were in fact discussing a poem.

Coleridge, a follower of Rousseau and Paine, was then trying to earn a living by writing and lecturing. He opposed the war with France, and was believed by the authorities to have democratic sympathies. The fact that he owned a printing press – perfect for publishing seditious literature – was highly suspicious. Nevertheless, agent Walsh thought Mr Poole, a philanthropist, was the most 'dangerous' democrat of the circle. Poole had established a 'Poor Man's Club' for '150 poor men' in the town and he was also a close friend of John Thelwall, who had by now moved on to Bristol. (Walsh knew this because he had seen a letter with Thelwall's new address).

The spy even reported servants' gossip about the Alfoxton group. Thomas Jones had been asked to wait at table for a dinner party for fourteen people at the manor house, including Poole and Coleridge. 'There was a little Stout Man with dark cropt Hair and wore a White Hat and Glasses [Thelwall] who after Dinner got up and talked so loud and was in such a Passion that Jones was frightened and did not like to go near them since.' Walsh then bribed Jones with a few shillings to get a job as a gardener at Alfoxton, so that he could find out more. The Wordsworths' female servant told Jones that, 'Her Master was a Phylosopher'. Walsh concluded his letter by saying that Thelwall was expected to return soon to Alfoxton.[20]

The Bow Street Runner spent several days tracking Coleridge and Wordsworth; he hid for hours listening to their conversations. The two poets often rested on their favourite seat by the seashore at Kilve, discussing poetry and philosophy. Walsh's activities were 'utterly unsuspected' by them, for as Coleridge said later, 'how indeed *could* such a suspicion enter our fancies?'

At first Walsh was alarmed, Coleridge claimed: 'He fancied, that we were aware of our danger; for he often heard me talk about one *Spy Nozy*, which he was inclined to interpret of himself, and of a remarkable feature belonging to him'. Finally Walsh realized that Spy Nozy was 'the name of a man [the philosopher Spinoza (1632–1677)] who had made a book and lived long ago'. On one occasion Walsh waylaid Coleridge as he walked home from Alfoxton, and chatted to him 'in a democrat way in order to draw me out'. But the poet convinced the spy that he 'was no friend to Jacobinism'.

One of the local magistrates, still convinced there was a nest of vipers in their midst, questioned the pub landlord while Walsh was present. The landlord quickly reassured them of Coleridge's good character: 'Why, folks do say, your Honour! as how that he is a Poet, and that he is going to put Quantock and all about here in print.' The magistrate was not easily convinced, but Walsh had heard enough to conclude that the two poets were not dangerous and his investigation was finished. According to Coleridge, he stoutly declared that the two poets were 'as good subjects, for aught he could discover to the contrary, as any in His Majesty's dominions'.[21]

For a short time, the Romantic poets had been in real danger of being arrested and imprisoned. Instead Coleridge, who learned of the tale through the pub landlord, gained a wonderful after-dinner story with which to entertain his guests. Wordsworth treated the whole affair as a storm in a teacup, but the owner of Alfoxton was very angry when he heard rumours that his tenants had been 'fingered' as possible Jacobins. The Wordsworths were forced to leave Alfoxton shortly afterwards.

Chapter Three

Ireland Ablaze!

In Ireland, suspicious persons were treated in a far more brutal fashion than Wordsworth and Coleridge had been in England. Spies and informers played a crucial role in Ireland throughout this blood-stained era. The readiness of Irishmen to betray and spy on their neighbours led to Marquess Cornwallis, Viceroy of Ireland from 1798 to 1801, dubbing them 'the most corrupt people under heaven'.[1]

Although Dublin Castle received intelligence on the United Irishmen from at least 1796 onwards, if not earlier, it needed concrete evidence before it could proceed against the rebel group's more prominent members. When Mr Wickham, the Superintendent of Aliens at the Alien Office, was made Under-Secretary of State at the Home Department in late 1797, he put more spies in place to uncover the leading conspirators.

Careless talk could cost lives even amongst family members. James Tandy, son of the famous United Irish leader Napper Tandy, was a terrible blabber-mouth. Little did he realize that whenever he discussed his father's movements, the information was relayed straight to Dublin Castle by the spy Lawrence McNally. However, it was difficult for the Castle's spies to infiltrate the United Irishmen from top to bottom, owing to the localized and secret nature of the organization, parts of which are still obscure even today.

There was a complex structure of local societies within the United Irishmen, partially supervised by 'baronial', county and district committees. The four provinces of Ulster, Leinster, Munster and Connaught each had a Subordinate Directory of just two or three members, who served on a provincial committee which supervised the county and district committees:

A "General Executive Directory" composed of five persons, was elected by the provincial directories; but the election of this directory was so managed, that none but the secretaries of the provincial directories knew on whom the election fell. It was made by ballot, but not reported to the electors; the appointment was notified only to those on whom the election devolved; and the executive directory...exercised the supreme...command of the whole body of the union, which by these secret modes of election, was kept utterly ignorant who were the persons to whom this implicit obedience was paid.[2]

Because of the way in which each local group was structured, even if a spy became a member and was elected to the provincial directory, this would not help him discover who was on the executive directory. The chiefs of the directories or committees changed constantly, too, as members were imprisoned or arrested, or fled the country during early 1797, when the government began to crack down on its opponents in Ulster.

In addition to Lawrence McNally, two more spies played a crucial role in the government's fight against the United Irishmen: Samuel Turner and Thomas Reynolds. Turner was a trusted member of the group's inner circle and he took a leading role in their plans. He also acted as a local contact in Hamburg for United Irishmen who had fled there, and was friends with rebel leader Lord Edward Fitzgerald and his wife Pamela. (Hamburg was then a free port and an important stopping-place for travellers going to and from the Continent).

Turner, using the aliases of Furnes (or Furness) and Richardson, sent information to Pitt's government via Lord Downshire, an Irish peer. It was almost certainly Turner who reported Fitzgerald's negotiations with the French Directory in the summer of 1796 to the authorities, prior to Hoche's disastrous expedition that December (see chapter 2). Turner covered his tracks as a spy so successfully that his treachery was not discovered for decades, when late in Queen Victoria's reign, the author W.F. Fitzpatrick pieced together clues within the state papers held at the Dublin Castle archives.

The Irish government's spies did not know one another's identities unless they happened to work together on a mission. Francis Higgins, a newspaper editor and spy who did not realize that Samuel Turner was a government mole, warned Dublin Castle in early June 1797 that Turner had sent letters from Portsmouth encouraging the mutinous seamen there to break into open rebellion. Higgins and his fellow spy Francis Magan did not know that McNally was a government spy, either, so they reported his dealings with the United Irishmen to their superiors as a matter of course. This meant that the authorities could cross-check each spy's reports for accuracy.

A Rebel Priest

In 1797 Lawrence McNally warned the government of the suspicious activities of many suspected Irish rebels, including: Father James O'Coigley; Arthur McMahon, a Presbyterian minister from County Down; and Arthur O'Connor, editor of the *Dublin Press*. Father O'Coigley (or Quigley) was a Roman Catholic priest and his movements were of special interest to Westminster and Dublin. This mild-mannered and big-boned man, almost 6ft tall, with grey eyes and grey hair, played a pivotal role in recruiting support for the United Irishmen on the British mainland.

During the summer of 1797, O'Coigley and McMahon set up rebel societies in London and north-west England (see chapter 4) along the same lines as the United Irish groups in their native Ireland. Next, the two priests visited their countrymen exiled in Paris, but they could not get any hard information regarding the ongoing negotiations with the French Directory. They seemingly fell out with Lewins, the official United Irish envoy (which undermined his credibility with the French), before they returned to England in mid-December 1797.

O'Coigley visited Dublin early the following year and met with rebels Dr William James McNevin and Lord Edward Fitzgerald, who were now planning the Irish rebellion. The government spy Francis Magan kept tabs on Father O'Coigley while he was in Dublin. In February 1798, the priest returned to England and travelled to London on a secret mission, using the aliases 'Captain Jones' and 'Fivey'. While in London he held several meetings with another United Irishman, Arthur O'Connor, a 'stout-built' man with 'dark eyes and eyebrows, black hair and whiskers',[3] who acted as liaison between the English, Scottish and Irish secret societies. O'Coigley begged O'Connor to come with him to France and lend support to the invasion plans. He wanted O'Connor to replace Lewins, now unjustly suspected of being a spy because of Samuel Turner's clandestine activities.

O'Connor also called on another United Irishman, John Binns, and asked him for help with their mission. Arthur O'Connor urgently needed to get to France, but the war made sailing between the two countries almost impossible without government permission. A smuggler's ship or a privateer was the only option. Binns agreed to travel to the Kent coast to arrange a passage to France for O'Connor and O'Coigley. Binns found a pilot at Margate willing to take the two Irishmen to France, and met O'Coigley and O'Connor at the port. Their luggage was a dead giveaway, as it comprised an immense quantity of baggage, as well as swords, pistols, and military accoutrements. John Binns thought that the locals must have alerted the authorities when they saw the cart, but in fact the government already knew of the rebels' movements from Samuel Turner.

Early on the morning of 28 February 1798, two Bow Street Runners, Edward Fugion and John Revett (who had been following O'Coigley and O'Connor), arrived accompanied by a party of light-horsemen. They arrested John Binns, Father O'Coigley, Arthur O'Connor, Jeremiah Leary (O'Connor's servant), and another Irishman, John Allen. They were searched and all their papers seized; then they were taken to Bow Street police office for questioning. There the five men were charged with high treason and inviting a French invasion.

At the Irishmen's trial in Maidstone on 21 May, the Bow Street Runners produced interesting evidence including a French passport belonging to O'Coigley, as well as a document detailing the 'Declaration, Resolutions and Constitution of the Societies of United Irishmen'. Under questioning, evidence appeared showing apparent links between the United Irishmen and the United Britons, another secret rebel society (see chapter 4). O'Coigley admitted that he had met two members of the United Britons, Dr Crossfield and Colonel Despard, but claimed that he did not know them very well.[4]

The government was in a quandary; it could not reveal all the evidence it possessed in court without jeopardising its spy Samuel Turner, who was still sending reports from the very heart of the United Irishmen's organization. The authorities brought into play a most unsavoury person, Frederick Dutton of Newry, to act as a Crown witness instead of Turner. Dutton was a common informer, a quartermaster in the Irish Royal Artillery, who had previously popped up as a Crown witness in two other treason trials. In return for a government sinecure, he testified that a letter to Lord Edward Fitzgerald (found at the nobleman's apartments in Leinster House) was in O'Connor's handwriting; he also confirmed that another suspicious letter was in the priest's handwriting.

O'Connor's letter to Fitzgerald seemed innocuous when taken at face value. However, when Arthur's luggage was forcibly opened at the secretary of state's office, a cipher was found in his razor-case containing a list of code-words used in the letters, with the key to their real meanings. For example, 'Williams' was the code-word for 'France' and '£1,000' really meant '1,000 men'.[5]

Despite his desperate situation, O'Connor was not without friends. Several prominent politicians from the government opposition – including Charles James Fox and Richard Brinsley Sheridan – appeared as character witnesses on his behalf. The eminent Irish politician, Henry Grattan, also stated that he believed that Arthur would never contemplate an invasion of his country.

O'Coigley was less fortunate. A letter from the 'Secret Committee of England' (the United Britons) to the 'Executive Directory of France' was found in his great-coat pocket, which proclaimed that: 'Affairs are now drawing to a great and awful crisis; tyranny…seems about to be buried in its own ruins. With the tyranny of England that of all Europe must fall.' The authors begged France to 'Haste then, Great Nation! to pour forth thy gigantic strength. Let our vile Despots feel thy avenging stroke…Go on! Englishmen will be ready to second your efforts.' The letter contained damning evidence of the spread of secret societies: 'We have already fraternised with the Secret Committees of the Irish and the Scotch, and a Delegate from each now sits with us.'[6]

O'Coigley's fate was sealed by this letter and he was found guilty of high treason. His solicitor Mr Foulkes tried to save him by asking the Duke of Portland for an urgent review of the two Bow Street Runners' testimony: 'Being informed that the evidence given by John Revett and Edward Fugion upon the trial of Mr James O'Coigley differed materially from that which they gave on their Examination at Bow Street before Richard Ford Esquire the Sitting Magistrate there.'[7] The priest only had a few days left to live, so

Foulkes also wrote to Richard Ford and the attorney general, but his efforts were unsuccessful.

As O'Coigley awaited execution, his jailers repeatedly begged him to implicate other United Irishmen, but he refused, even though he was promised a pardon in return. He never revealed the true author of that fatal letter. Father O'Coigley was executed on Pennington Heath on 7 June. George III graciously spared him the ordeal of being drawn and quartered. After he was hanged O'Coigley's head was severed, and his head and body were buried underneath the gallows.

However, to the government's chagrin, the priest's fellow defendants, including Arthur O'Connor were acquitted, even though they were deeply implicated in the secret pact with the French. John Binns, thanking his lucky stars, went to ground in the Midlands and stayed with some friends. Yet, thanks to Turner's information, the government was convinced that Arthur O'Connor was too dangerous to be at large. He was promptly re-arrested and sent to Dublin on a charge of high treason.

Insurrection!

While the authorities were suppressing the United Irishmen's activities on mainland Britain, great swathes of Ireland were ablaze. The Irish government's brutal handling of its people had proved the final straw. For months the Protestant Ascendancy, aided by the native Irish militia, had subjected ordinary folk to the most horrendous tortures, ostensibly with the aim of putting down potential rebels.

Martial law was declared over the whole of Ulster in March 1797. Then Lord Pelham (Chief Secretary for Ireland) gave the British commander General Lake *carte blanche* to deal with any outbreaks in the province, without waiting for permission from magistrates. Lake's severe measures successfully curtailed the United Irishmen's activities in Ulster, and as a result, Leinster and Dublin became rebel strongholds.

In January 1798, the people of Queen's County began fighting back against the authorities; arms were stolen, and magistrates attacked and killed. The Irish army was now completely out of control. Sir Ralph Abercromby, the Commander-in-Chief, publicly accused it of being 'formidable to everyone but the enemy' in February 1798.[8] Not only were the soldiers undisciplined, they were also dotted around the Irish countryside in small groups, rendering them virtually useless if French troops landed. The Irish gentry, many of whom had sons in the army, were outraged by Abercromby's comments, which he was forced to retract.

Despite the political difficulties caused by keeping Abercromby at his post, he and General Lake were sent to stamp out the disturbances. Whole areas were punished and forced to provide free board and lodging for the Irish soldiers, who commandeered any supplies they wanted. Large groups of the soldiery ran riot, which simply added more recruits to the republican cause.

Then the Dublin government had an amazing stroke of luck. As the plans of the United Irishmen matured, Thomas Reynolds, a member of the Leinster Provincial Committee, contacted the government to say that he had vital information for them. Reynolds, a Dublin silk-mercer and United Irish colonel, originally joined the movement because he wanted Catholic emancipation. He had recently purchased Kilkea Castle, in Kildare, and had family connections with both Lord Edward Fitzgerald and Wolfe Tone, who was his brother-in-law.

Thomas claimed that he had withdrawn from the United Irishmen for a short time to deal with some personal affairs. Then Lord Edward Fitzgerald asked Reynolds to take over some of his duties on the local committee of the United Irishmen, as Fitzgerald was worried that the government was spying on him. Reynolds (reluctantly, so he said) agreed. When Reynolds attended a United Irish meeting near Dublin in February 1798, he discovered to his horror that an armed insurrection was imminent. The uprising would begin with the death or capture of eighty members of the Irish government. A French invasion in support of the rebels was expected daily. This was high treason and, if caught, Reynolds could hang.

Eager to escape his predicament, Reynolds consulted a family friend and Dublin merchant, Mr Cope, who had connections with the Irish government. Cope introduced him to Lord Pelham. Reynolds agreed to turn informer providing he was guaranteed immunity from prosecution, and never asked to give evidence in court.

Meanwhile, the authorities were still getting regular updates from Samuel Turner. He gave them the names of the top men in the United Irishmen's Executive Directory, then based in Leinster: wealthy Dublin merchant Oliver Bond; newspaper editor Arthur O'Connor; Dr McNevin; Lord Edward Fitzgerald; and Thomas Addis Emmet. Following information from Reynolds that the United Irishmen had gained many new recruits, and that a meeting of the secret committee was planned, the government acted swiftly. On 12 March fourteen members of the Executive Directory were arrested at Bond's house, except for O'Connor and Fitzgerald, who were absent. Reynolds gave the society's secret password to the authorities, to make it easier for soldiers to gain entry to the house. The day after Bond's arrest, Reynolds visited Oliver Bond's wife and baby to express his sympathy.

Reynolds was now in deep trouble, as the United Irishmen suspected he had betrayed them, and he was desperate to emigrate. He was in danger from both sides, because the local militia thought he was a rebel and arrested him, unaware that he was a government spy. Reynolds faced summary execution by court-martial, but he contrived to contact his employers in Dublin Castle, and was taken to the safety of the Castle by armed guard. The game was up: Reynolds was now useless as an undercover agent. He agreed to give evidence against the United Irishmen, on condition that his family was given protection. He was well paid for his treachery, however; by March 1799, Reynolds had received £5,000 of secret service money.

The arrest of the committee mortally wounded the United Irishmen. Lord Edward Fitzgerald was now their de facto leader, aided by an attorney, John Sheares. Yet Fitzgerald was a weak leader, despite his personal charm – and little did he realise that his 'friend' Samuel Turner was betraying his every move.

The spy Francis Higgins was also busy sending information about Fitzgerald to Dublin Castle. In addition, Higgins had recruited Francis Magan, a Catholic barrister who was down on his luck. Magan, or 'M.' as he was referred to in the spy reports, was a United Irishman and knew Fitzgerald well. After the committee members' arrests, Magan joined the newly re-formed secret committee, and sometime in early May began reporting on Fitzgerald's movements.

Fitzgerald was a marked man – a reward of £1,000 had been offered for his head. Almost everything was now ready for the insurrection; nearly a quarter of a million men had sworn to live and die in the great cause. The Dublin, Meath, Kildare areas, and the villages of the Wicklow mountains seethed with energy. The rebellion was set for 23 May 1798: Fitzgerald's grand plan was for a massive attack on Dublin with all his men. In the meantime, the aristocrat moved from one safe house to another, hoping to foil the authorities. On the night of 17 May, Fitzgerald and his bodyguard hurried to a house at Usher's Island in Dublin, close to where Magan lived. When the spy realized that Fitzgerald was in the area, he alerted Higgins, who passed on the information to the authorities.

Two days later, Major Sirr the town-major of Dublin, Captain Swan the assistant town-major, Captain Ryan, and 200 soldiers went to arrest Fitzgerald. Swan and Ryan crept first into his room, but Fitzgerald leapt to his feet and fought 'like a tiger'.[9] Swan, after receiving several stab wounds, fired his pistol at Fitzgerald and wounded him slightly. Then Swan hurried downstairs to fetch Sirr and his men. Meanwhile, Captain Ryan lunged at Fitzgerald with a sword-cane and inflicted several wounds. When Sirr arrived he saw their desperate fight and fired his gun at Fitzgerald.

Even then, several men were needed to subdue Fitzgerald sufficiently to get him out of the house and into custody at Dublin Castle. He died about three weeks later from his wounds. Wolfe Tone remembered him as a 'gallant fellow…His memory will live forever in the heart of every honest Irishman'.[10]

Fitzgerald's capture enriched his betrayers: Higgins received £1,000 of secret service money and an annual stipend of £300, while his accomplice Francis Magan also gained a £300 pension.

Lord Fitzgerald's death was another dreadful blow to the United Irishmen. Soon afterwards they received another setback when the government arrested and later hanged two more important rebels, John Sheares and his brother Henry, thanks to another spy. The Irish government must have thought that the rebellion would now wither away.

But atrocities by the Orangemen and Irish soldiers re-ignited the smouldering embers of revolution. People's huts were burnt down; women were raped; men were flogged until they died; and some were half-hanged to make them confess to 'crimes' their torturers claimed they had committed. 'Pitch-capping' was a particularly nasty form of torture, in which a linen cap covered with hot pitch was placed on the victim's head, then set on fire. The counties of Wicklow, Kildare and Carlow suffered the most, and these horrors incited wild rumours that all Catholics would soon be wiped out.

On 23 May, the day set for the rising, United Irish attacks took place in Meath, Kildare and the outskirts of Dublin. These rebels were soon vanquished but, as word quickly spread, the oppressed peasantry seized the moment. Martial law was declared over all Ireland. The main battles of the great rebellion were fought at Arklow, Enniscorthy, Ross, and Vinegar Hill.

The civil war was exacerbated by sectarian animosities, and sickening atrocities were perpetrated, according to Wolfe Tone's son William:

'The country blazed with nightly conflagrations, and resounded with the shrieks of torture; neither age nor sex was spared, and the bayonets of the military sent men, women and children, naked and houseless, to starve in the bogs and fastnesses; those who trusted to the faith of capitulations were surrounded and slaughtered by dragoons in the very act of laying down their arms; and no citizen, no matter how innocent and inoffensive, could deem himself secure from informers.'[11]

No quarter was given by either side to combatants and civilians alike. Government forces massacred prisoners and suspects at Carnew and Dunlavin, while at Gibbet Rath when over 300 rebels tried to surrender they were cut down without mercy. At Scullabogue victorious rebels burned to death nearly 200 loyalist prisoners, including women and children. The viciousness of the government forces served only to inflame the rebellion, while the rebels' ferocity further inflamed loyalist depredations. As news of the horrors reached Britain, the government's patience with Ireland's Viceroy, Lord Camden, finally ran out. In late June, Lord Cornwallis, a humane and brilliant commander, was appointed Viceroy in Camden's stead, with orders to quell the rebellion, assisted by reinforcements from England.

As Wolfe Tone's son later wrote, the small, disorganized and localized rebel outbreaks were inevitably no match for the government forces, no matter how gallantly they fought. Cornwallis, meanwhile, was determined to pacify the country, and hasten a Union with Britain. He pushed through an amnesty for the ordinary rebels, and ordered the local justices and yeomanry to stop flogging and hanging people without trial. One by one, the rebels took advantage of the amnesty and surrendered. By early August it seemed that the insurrection was over and it was just a question of dealing with the aftermath.

Invasion!

While Ireland burned, the French were nowhere to be seen. Unfortunately, General Hoche, an ardent republican, had died and his replacement, Napoleon Bonaparte, had set his sights on the conquest of Egypt. When news of the Irish insurrection reached France in late May, Wolfe Tone frantically urged the Directory to help his suffering countrymen. Dozens of Irish refugees also arrived by boat, bearing heart-rending tales of bloodshed. But the French had no arms, money, men or ships to spare.

Tone, anxiously reading the news reports, wrote in his diary: 'If the Irish can hold out till winter…the French will assist them effectually. All I dread is, they may be overpowered by that time.'[12] Wolfe Tone's fears were justified: the French did not arrive until far too late.

Three invasion forces were eventually sent. The first was commanded by the hot-headed General Humbert, who had been present at the Bantry Bay debacle. Humbert, moved by the Irish refugees' stories, decided to launch an invasion on his own authority, before everything was ready. He sailed with Tone's brother Matthew, and two other Irishmen, Bartholomew Teeling and Sullivan. Humbert took 1,000 men and muskets, and a small amount of artillery. His ships reached Killala Bay, Connaught on 22 August 1798. At first Humbert's expedition went well. He won a notable victory against General Lake's British forces at Castlebar, helped by the fact that the Irish militia regiments ran away. The news of Humbert's arrival gave fresh hope to the republicans, and disturbances began afresh.

The Home Office later received a confidential report via Lord Castlereagh (acting Chief Secretary for Ireland) about the Irish landings. (It's not clear whether this is a report from a spy who had posed as a rebel, or a rebel's confession). Michael Burke joined the French troops at Castlebar on 31

August. He claimed that 'Five or six thous^d [sic] of the Country People' had joined the French forces. They were kitted out with blue and white uniforms, and caps or helmets. Their numbers were swelled by deserters from the 'Longford & Kilkenny' regiments, who thought that the French would protect them as they were Roman Catholics.

According to Burke, the French planned to march from Castlebar to Sligo, then proceed north to Dublin. Burke also reported several conversations with Matthew Tone, who explained that two more landings were planned: 'for the purpose of invading Ireland in the parts least protected – that his Brother [Wolfe Tone] was to come with one, and seemed rather to think that he must have arrived by this time, and N. Tandy with another'.[13]

Burke left the French army at Collooney, just before it was attacked by the Limerick militia, which was easily overpowered by Humbert. Then the French general heard that Longford and Westmeath had risen, and hurriedly turned his forces to aid them.

Burke's report was accurate. United Irish leader Napper Tandy was indeed on his way, yet his outing proved somewhat inglorious. Tandy and General Rey had sailed from Dunkirk on the *Anacreon*, one of the fastest-sailing corvettes in the French navy. They brought just over 300 French soldiers, and a large contingent of United Irish refugees who wanted to resume the fight. They arrived on 16 September at the island of Rutland, off Donegal. Unknown to Tandy, one of his shipmates, George Orr, (code-name 'O'), was a spy for the British government.

Napper Tandy had boasted to the French Directory that tens of thousands of Irishmen would flock to his banner upon his arrival. The Irish flag was raised, and proclamations were issued to assure the locals that the soldiers had come to 'break your fetters, and restore you to the blessings of liberty'.[14]

But Tandy was on his native soil for less than a day. He received devastating news: Humbert had been soundly defeated by Lord Cornwallis at Ballinamuck (near Longford) and forced to surrender. The expedition was doomed. Tandy decided to drown his sorrows, according to Orr's secret report: 'He intoxicated himself to such a degree as to be incapable of getting to the boat, and p–d on the shoulders of those who carried him to it.'[15] The *Anacreon* sailed away.

Four weeks after Tandy's luckless landing, Admiral Bompart's fleet arrived. This was the main French invasion force, commanded by General Hardy, with Wolfe Tone in the *Hoche*. The fleet set off from Brest on 16 September, following news of Humbert's initial success. However, the French did not make landfall. When their ships reached the entrance to Lough Swilly (County Donegal) on 11 October, they were foiled by the arrival of the British fleet, commanded by Sir John Borlase Warren. After a terrific battle, Warren defeated the French and Wolfe Tone was captured. A few days earlier, Britons had been overwhelmed with joy at the news of Nelson's victory over Bonaparte in the Battle of the Nile. For the time being, the French navy was no longer a threat.

One notable absentee from the Ireland landings was the spy Samuel Turner. Terrified that he would be assassinated if he set foot in his native land, he stayed safely on the Continent. He had reason, as many state informers were quietly murdered during these perilous times.

Other informers played an ignoble role in the aftermath of the rebellion, too. Lord Cornwallis put an amnesty in place for the rebels, but it could be overset for those proven to have been among the rebel leaders or found guilty of murder in a court of law. In County Wicklow, the turncoat Bridget Nolan ('Croppy Biddy') of Carnew became infamous for her willingness to swear away the lives of any rebels or Catholics the local magistrates wanted to bring to 'justice'. According to a local Catholic monk and historian, Luke Cullen, Biddy was well-known locally for her loose morals and drinking; she rode with the rebel army and took part in many 'deeds of iniquity' during the insurrection.

After the rebellion Biddy began drinking with the loyalists in local pubs, and the magistrates decided to make use of her as an informer and perjurer. 'She was now dressed like a lady, with habit and skirt, hat and feather, and a prancing palfrey was placed at her disposal.'[16] She rode around the countryside at the head of a party of soldiers and pointed out former, or alleged, rebels to them, later giving evidence against them in court. Biddy received an annual salary of £22 15s (roughly equivalent to £2,500 today) from the secret service coffers for her services. When it became clear that her evidence was unreliable, commander Lord Cornwallis intervened and reduced the severity of the court sentences on some of her victims – too late for those who had already been executed.

Meanwhile, the surviving rebel Irish leaders were awaiting execution for high treason at Newgate Gaol in Dublin. After the death of the Sheares brothers and other United Irish leaders, in late July 1798 the state prisoners made an extraordinary offer to Lord Cornwallis and Lord Castlereagh. Arthur O'Connor, Thomas Addis Emmet, Dr McNevin and Oliver Bond promised to make a public statement of their guilt, and the true aims of the United Irishmen, in return for their lives. Bond, however, died in his jail cell under mysterious circumstances while these negotiations were taking place.

The United Irishmen's declaration of intent caused great embarrassment to the British government's Whig opponents, like Charles James Fox, who had previously welcomed some of them as personal friends. Those rebels still at large, including Matthew Tone, were disgusted and 'reprobated them for betraying the cause & turning informers for the sake of saving their lives'.[17]

The Irish government had assured the rebel leaders that after their confession they could migrate to America, providing they never returned to Europe. America, however, refused to take them, so in early December Lord Castlereagh informed the prisoners that some would be exiled to a neutral country on the Continent, although fifteen of them – including O'Connor and Dr McNevin – could not yet be freed. These unlucky prisoners were sent to Fort George in Scotland until the government felt it was safe to release them. The spy Samuel Turner had now joined them, and seemingly fomented discord amongst his fellow prisoners. They were not freed for over three years.

Napper Tandy and other United Irish refugees fled to Hamburg (neutral territory, where they should have been beyond the reach of the British government) but they were arrested by the authorities and deported to Ireland as a favour to Britain. Tandy was later tried for treason, found guilty and sentenced to death, but as he was no longer considered a threat he was allowed to emigrate to France.

Wolfe Tone was not so lucky. In November 1798 he was found guilty by a court-martial. Strictly speaking, this trial was illegal, as Tone was no longer a British subject – he was a soldier of the French Republic and therefore not bound by British or Irish laws. Tone declared that he had sacrificed his life 'in the cause of justice and freedom'. He asked to be executed by firing squad, but the Irish government refused, and he was condemned to a traitor's death instead. Tone tried to cheat the hangman by cutting his own throat with a penknife, but failed to sever the artery before he was discovered. A surgeon sewed up the wound, but Tone could not be saved; he took eight days to die. 'I am sorry I have been so bad an anatomist,' he joked shortly before he expired.[18]

The rebellion took a dreadful toll on Ireland. Several towns lay in ruins; tens of thousands had been killed or injured, and many others executed or exiled by the authorities. There was a great outpouring of impoverished Irish to the British mainland, seeking employment. Ironically, the insurrection directly brought about the 1800 Act of Union between Ireland and Great Britain; Prime Minister William Pitt had achieved his goal at last. The dream of an independent Ireland was seemingly dead and buried. Ireland no longer had its own parliament; it was ruled directly by Westminster. The issue of Catholic emancipation was shelved and George III's continued refusal to allow its introduction led to Pitt's resignation the following year.

Robert Emmet's Rebellion

But the spirit of republicanism was not yet dead. During the ensuing years, the republican cause was hamstrung by a Catch-22 situation. The United Irishmen refused to countenance another uprising without guaranteed French support, while the French refused to commit any more men or ships unless the republicans could muster sufficient forces for a widespread uprising.

Historians disagree as to how much advance warning the government had from its spies in Ireland concerning Robert Emmet's Dublin rebellion in July 1803. (Robert was Thomas Addis Emmet's younger brother.) Emmet's rising was originally meant to take place in conjunction with a planned insurrection in England led by Colonel Despard (see chapter 4). According to United Irishman James Hope, Despard contacted William Dowdall, a veteran of the 1798 Irish rebellion, to ask him to organize a rebellion in Ireland in concert with the one he was then plotting in London.

The Irish exiles in France heard of Dowdall's plans and in October 1802 Robert Emmet arrived in Dublin to discover how far advanced they were. Emmet then took over the planning of the insurrection. The idea was to attack Dublin Castle and the artillery barracks, seize the Viceroy, his family, and the Privy Council, then hold them as hostages. Emmet expected hundreds of men from Wexford, Kildare, and Wicklow to flock to his aid. Towards the end of March 1803, Emmet began assembling men and arms in earnest.

The Home Office had already received some information of a plot from Bolton in Lancashire, but it was either deemed unreliable or simply not passed on to the Dublin authorities. On 8 April 1803, Bolton magistrate Colonel Fletcher wrote to the Home Office about a report from his spy 'B' (Bent). An Irish delegate had visited Manchester on 3 April, to see why the citizens there were so lacking in zeal for the cause. The Irishman said that the rebels in Ireland 'were never more numerous and never more determined'.[19] He also claimed that some delegates from France had recently arrived in the west of Ireland, and the rebels intended to rise whether war was resumed with France or not. (The short-lived Peace of Amiens fizzled out in May 1803, when England declared war on France.)

Napoleon's forces were thought to be planning an invasion of Britain that autumn and Emmet's rising was planned to coincide with a French landing, possibly on England's south coast. However, Emmet's plans were blown wide open when some stores of gunpowder and ammunition exploded in Patrick Street, Dublin. Emmet had no choice but to bring forward his rebellion. On 23 July, Emmet and his associates assembled in Thomas Street, their swords drawn. But only about 100–200 men joined them, and the would-be rebels in other counties would not stir without help from France. Emmet's insurgents attacked the barracks, and some soldiers were killed, but with such insufficient numbers the rebellion was doomed, and it was quickly snuffed out.

Robert Emmet was tried for high treason on 7 September 1803. After he had been sentenced to death by hanging, Emmet declared in a famous speech, 'I have parted with everything that was dear to me in this life for my country's cause.'[20] And at his side throughout the trial was his defence counsel and dear friend: Lawrence McNally.

Chapter Four

Inside The Secret Societies

The Home Office gathered intelligence on several groups of democrats in Great Britain during the late 1790s and early 1800s, including the United Irishmen, United Englishmen, the United Britons, and United Scotsmen. The relationships between these groups are not easy to untangle, but we can gain a fascinating glimpse of their clandestine activities from the Home Office spy and witness reports.

The Origins of a Conspiracy

Many Irishmen fled to Britain in the mid-1790s, following their government's brutal crackdown on the United Irishmen and the Orangemen's persecution of the Catholics. These dissident Irishmen tried to drum up recruits in London, north-west England, and the manufacturing districts of Scotland, which all had significant Irish populations. By late 1796 London had its own group of United Irishmen.

Over the next few months, O'Coigley and John Binns founded groups called the United Britons and United Englishmen in London, on the tried-and-tested Irish model. As Binns and his brother Benjamin were members of the London Corresponding Society, the United Englishmen may have been a splinter group from the LCS. Whatever the truth, O'Coigley and Binns wanted to create district groups in those coastal areas most exposed to potential invasion forces.

The use of names such as 'United Englishmen' and 'United Scotsmen', etc., was designed to appeal to their members' patriotism, and perhaps also to disguise their links with the Irish rebels. One spy later reported that, 'The Societies were to go under the Names of the united Englishmen Irishmen & Scotchmen but it had been overruled at present not to bear the name of united Irishmen as it was thought not prudent their Country being in a state of rebellion.'[1]

One of the United Irishmen's chief contacts in England included Colonel Despard (1751–1803), who has gone down in history as the deluded leader of a wildly impractical, hopeless scheme. However, Despard was probably just one link in a whole network of rebels across Britain, Ireland and France. Despard's London-based group, the United Britons, planned to support the Irish in a co-ordinated effort. Simultaneous uprisings in England, Scotland and Ireland, coupled with a French invasion, would have put enormous pressure on the British government's forces.

In the London area, the United Englishmen had forty divisions, twenty of which met regularly. The United Englishmen set up 'free-and-easy' clubs for the working classes, possibly as a recruiting measure, where men could have a good night out for the princely sum of one penny: 'Songs were sung, and toasts given, and language held, of the most seditious nature.'[2]

As the authorities later discovered, several corresponding societies in the provinces transformed themselves into local divisions of the United Englishmen. Manchester allegedly had a large organization, with fifty divisions (later increased to eighty), which sent delegates to Yorkshire, Derbyshire, Nottinghamshire and Cheshire. A faction also existed in Liverpool. As all these groups expected the Home Office to intercept their mail: 'They avoided, as far as possible, the keeping [of] any papers; used ciphers or mysterious words, in the few writings that passed between them, and principally carried on their intercourse by agents, who went from place to place, and were recognised by signs, which were frequently changed.'[3]

The government believed that 'United Britons' was just another name for the United Englishmen, yet the two organizations appear to have had separate leaders at some dates. To add to the confusion, some Irishmen were members of both groups, and according to a reliable state mole, the United Irishmen had no Englishmen as members, perhaps as a defence against spies.

Whatever the precise composition of these groups, they were extremely active. The United Irishmen and United Britons set up a secret central committee in London to act as a meeting place for delegates from the provinces, Scotland and Ireland, and to co-ordinate English and Irish groups in the capital. The secretary was Dr Richard Crossfield, a former

LCS member, and the committee also included the Binns brothers and Colonel Despard.

The United Irishmen's 1797 plan had been that, as soon as the enemy fleet from the Texel landed in Ireland, 'An insurrection should be attempted in London', headed by Despard. The King and Privy Council were to be murdered, and '40,000 men' would be 'ready to turn out' in an uprising.[4] The Dutch fleet's defeat at Camperdown that autumn scuppered that plan, however.

Early in 1798 the United Britons sent three delegates to the Irish National Committee in Dublin: the Binns brothers and Father O'Coigley. As the Home Office later noted, this visit was: 'The first time when the name of United Britons seems to have been publicly assumed.'[5] They took with them an address declaring that the United Britons would do their utmost 'to promote the Emancipation of both Countries'.[6]

The government's claims of a cross-border connection between the United Irishmen, United Englishmen and United Britons were given some backing by informer and witness evidence from the Manchester area. It's difficult to judge how many members of these local societies were really revolutionaries, but owing to the Irish dimension the government had little option but to take these reports seriously.

The Manchester Connection

The leading United Englishmen in Manchester were local shopkeeper William Cheetham, Robert Gray, 'a low man and rather pock-marked', who later turned informer, and James Dixon, a weaver and cotton spinner.[7] According to Dixon's later testimony, the United Englishmen in Manchester sprang from the former Manchester Corresponding Society, originally founded by James Shaw of Deansgate, an LCS member from London. However the Manchester Corresponding Society received a major set-back when the 'mechanics' fell out with the 'gentlemen' members.

When Shaw returned from a trip to Yorkshire, where he had been giving political lectures (perhaps raising recruits for the United Englishmen), he tried to rally the members. A 'great meeting' was held at St John's churchyard, at which Shaw and Thomas Walker, a well-known Radical, were present, and subsequently membership of 'the Societies' increased again. Dixon claimed that he became a member of the United Englishmen around that time.[8]

Dixon, a tall man with black hair and grey eyes, was originally from Belfast. As he regularly travelled back and forth between Manchester and Ireland, he was an ideal messenger, carrying papers between the United Irishmen and the United Englishmen in north-west England. Robert Gray, who belonged to another Manchester division of the United Englishmen, paid Dixon's travelling expenses for one of these Ireland visits, which may explain why the rebels decided Gray was a trustworthy contact. Dixon brought back 400 copies of the 'Oath, and Test, and Rules of the United Englishmen', and news that the United Irishmen now had '400,570' men ready, and '19,500 of the Army'.[9]

The Manchester group had links with Scotland, too. Dixon said that a delegate from Glasgow, a Mr Hardy, had recently met him at Manchester, along with O'Hare (or O'Hara), a lame Irishman he knew well as they were both freemasons from the same lodge. Hardy and O'Hare had quizzed Dixon, 'respecting the state of the United Men at Manchester'. Dixon told them that UE membership in 'Manchester was falling off', which upset Hardy.[10]

Father O'Coigley was the key delegate who travelled between all the different groups in Britain. In June 1797, Father O'Coigley and O'Hare stayed in a Manchester pub for several nights. During his visit O'Coigley held separate meetings with Dixon and Gray.[11] O'Coigley, wearing military dress and using the name 'Captain Jones', asked to see Robert Gray, as he had heard that he 'was an active person in the cause of democracy'. The two men exchanged a secret countersign (drawing a hand over one eye), and the passwords 'Unity' and 'Truth'. After more secret countersigns, O'Coigley showed Gray two letters, one of which was a letter of introduction for the priest from the national committee of Ireland (United Irishmen) to the French people.

The other paper was a confidential letter to the Manchester group, which reported that two men had been shot in Ireland, 'one an informer', another a 'Gentleman' who had been zealously prosecuting the United Irishmen. The letter claimed that: 'Three hundred thousand United Irishmen and nineteen thousand and a half of the army' were ready to rise up, but 'no good would be done until they should assassinate the Petty Tyrants of Manchester [the magistrates]…and then they would fear as they did in Ireland.'

The priest wanted the Manchester group to raise money to buy arms, so that they would be ready to rise up when the French invaded. When Gray told him that 'the people was [sic] poor, and trade bad', O'Coigley said they must get some arms from Ireland, where there were plenty available. It must be done swiftly, O'Coigley explained, as soon he and Arthur O'Connor would visit France to make the final push for the invasion. He also told Gray that the French believed that once Ireland became a republic, it would 'revolutionize the other two kingdoms' (i.e. England and Scotland).[12]

Dixon and Gray may have liaised with William Cheetham, a leading United Englishman, on O'Coigley's behalf. Cheetham had been an active Manchester member for over a year. One of the men he tried to recruit was Samuel Patterson, a Salford auctioneer. As Patterson later claimed when questioned by the magistrates, he had refused to join, even though Cheetham promised that if 'an Invasion or Revolution took place' all his debts would be paid. Patterson knew that Cheetham and Robert Gray, a former employee of Cheetham's, were members of the United Englishmen, so when Cheetham asked him to join, he naturally wanted more details of what they were planning. Cheetham replied that he could not tell Patterson that 'until he had taken the oath'. Patterson wisely gave him the brush-off.[13]

At this time, the Manchester authorities had no idea that there was a rebel group of United Englishmen right under their noses. Then, in the spring of 1798, Robert Gray betrayed the cell to a local magistrate after a quarrel with William Cheetham. Gray gave names, addresses and physical descriptions of the United Englishmen to local magistrate Thomas Butterworth Bayley. Gray also said that Dixon had acted as a delegate from Manchester to the United Irishmen, and had recruited soldiers from the local barracks: 'there were 50 Stout Fellows…and he did not doubt but that they would make themselves a hundred.'[14] Dixon was a freemason, so he could call at the barracks without arousing suspicion.

Butterworth Bayley and his fellow magistrates were sceptical, so they asked a cavalryman, Sergeant Joseph Tankard, to infiltrate the United Englishmen to see if he could confirm Gray's story. When Tankard was duly sworn in, James Dixon asked the sergeant if he could get more soldiers to join them. Tankard's testimony was enough for the authorities, and arrests followed swiftly. In early April 1798, Samuel Patterson and two others were arrested and incarcerated in the New Bailey Prison at Salford. James Dixon, John Dodds, William Cheetham, and others were arrested, taken to London for questioning, and sent to Coldbath Fields Prison. As Habeas Corpus was then suspended, the government could hang on to the men for an indefinite period; Cheetham was not released until early 1801.

When James Dixon was arrested by Bow Street Runner James Reeves, at the 'Sign of the Archer' on Dale Street in Manchester, he was searched. Reeves found some printed papers containing the 'Declaration, Resolutions and Constitution of the Societies of United Englishmen', and another paper entitled 'Freedom Defended' in Dixon's coat pockets.[15] The 'Declaration' claimed that the society ostensibly wanted to effect change by legal means – parliamentary reform: 'For which Purpose we have agreed to form an association to be called the United Englishmen, under which name we pledge ourselves to our Country, and to each other, to persevere in *all legal means* [author's italics], till we have obtained the object of our Desire.'[16]

This was probably a front for their true insurrectionary aims, as an anonymous London informant, who had been a member of the United Englishmen for a year, said that it intended 'to form a republic thro' the means of the French'.[17] The oath taken by soldiers when joining the society (also amongst papers found when the arrests were made) certainly has a mutinous ring: 'In the awful presence of God A B do sware [sic] not [to] obey the Cornol [colonel] nor the Officors [sic] set over me but the Country [chiefs? illegible] or Committee then setting [sic] of United Inglishmen [sic] so help my God.'[18]

When William Cheetham was examined at Whitehall by Richard Ford, the Bow Street magistrate who oversaw intelligence-gathering in England, Cheetham denied point-blank that he was a United Englishman, a United Briton, or a member of 'any Society whatever'. He denied knowing O'Coigley, but admitted helping with a ten-pound subscription for a 'Roman Catholic priest in distress in London' called Fivey (one of O'Coigley's aliases), which Gray had asked him to organize.[19] Ford questioned him again a few weeks later, but Cheetham stoutly maintained his innocence: 'He has not violated any of the laws of his Country and has nothing to say in his Defence.'[20]

Gray's testimony also threw suspicion on other notable Manchester Radicals like Thomas Walker and William Cowdroy, and more 'persons of the Higher Order' at Manchester, as they too had given money for the supposedly impoverished priest.[21] The Lancashire arrests must have caused some finger-pointing locally, because Samuel Patterson sent a bellman round the Salford streets to announce to all and sundry that 'he was not the Informer'.[22]

Meanwhile, in Scotland the United Scotsmen, also formed along the same lines as the United Irishmen, had made some headway, especially in the Glasgow area. One member, George Mealmaker, was tried for sedition and transported.

The United Irishmen had apparently made some progress towards suborning the Scottish regiments, because during the third week of April 1798, a 'meanly-dressed' Irishman confided to a supposed confederate in Chester that: 'We have…gained over most of the Scotch Fencible regiments but we cannot make anything of the English regiments.' The Irishman added, almost as an afterthought, that it was: 'An unlucky affair, the Manchester business not succeeding.'[23]

Treasonable Practices

In London, however, the rebels' plans were gaining momentum. As noted earlier, the London Corresponding Society's original remit was a peaceful campaign for parliamentary reform. Yet according to an anonymous informant who had been a member of the LCS for five years, and served on the executive committee, its leaders now wanted a revolution.

In March 1798 there were at least seven groups of United Englishmen in the capital; one of their main meeting places was Furnival's Inn Cellar in Holborn. Thomas Evans, a print-colourist who lived in Plough Court, Fetter Lane, was one of the leading organizers, along with Alexander Galloway. Pikes were being forged in Pancras Place; the men distributed 'seditious Handbills' amongst the soldiers in Hyde Park; and members were encouraged to infiltrate the local militia.

When news of the arrests of the Margate five (see chapter 2) reached them, Thomas Evans and the other UE leaders discussed the possibility of killing the crown witnesses against the Irishmen, but decided against it, probably because it was a wholly impractical scheme. Nonetheless, they threatened 'to destroy Gray and Tankard' (the Manchester informers) and began 'making Enquiries how…they can get at them.' The informer who gave this information to Bow Street said that he would be killed if the United Englishmen ever found out he had spilled the beans.[24]

Evans was taken in during mid–March and he was considered such an important prisoner that the Duke of Portland was present for his interrogation. Evans admitted meeting Despard at the Holborn cellar, as well as Captain Jones (alias Father O'Coigley), but he had never seen Despard with Jones. Other visitors to the cellar were Dr Crossfield, one of the Binns brothers, and James Powell. Little did Evans realize that Powell was a government spy (possibly the anonymous informant mentioned earlier who reported the plot to kill Gray and Tankard).

Evans was released but did not enjoy his liberty for long. Four weeks after the arrest of the Margate five, the government made countrywide arrests. Over several days Evans, Despard, Crossfield and others were seized. Additional suspects were detained in Birmingham, Scotland and Ireland, as well as those in Lancashire.

On 20 April, Pitt's government suspended Habeas Corpus once again and five days later, Despard was committed to the House of Correction at Clerkenwell, under suspicion of 'treasonable practices'; Thomas Evans and John Bone were also imprisoned there, suspected of high treason. Benjamin Binns and Galloway found themselves in Newgate; Robert Thomas Crossfield was held in Tothill Fields Prison, suspected of 'high treason'; and Charles Pendrill, another LCS man, was imprisoned but later released.[25]

Daring Despard

By now Colonel Despard had plenty of reasons to hold a grudge against the establishment. The Irishman had formerly served with distinction in the British Army, as chief engineer to a youthful Captain Horatio Nelson (later the scourge of the French fleets) in an expedition against the Spanish Main. Despard commanded a successful and daring raid on the Black River of the Mosquito Shore. Later, Despard was given a government post as Superintendent at the Bay of Honduras, but owing to some political jealousies, was forced to return to London to defend his conduct.

After Whitehall kept him in suspense for two years while his case was reviewed, Despard's post in Honduras was abolished. He never received the expenses he was owed, so he got into financial difficulties and was imprisoned for debt in 1792. Despard had plenty of time to think about the state of British politics during the two years he spent in the King's Bench Prison. The government eventually admitted that all the alleged charges against him were baseless, but he had little chance of rebuilding his career and reputation. After his release, he joined the London Corresponding Society. Now he was back inside a cell again...

The Sons of Liberty

Spy reports reveal that several secret cells continued meeting in London during the summer of 1798, despite the springtime arrests. Some LCS members discussed the possibility of obtaining arms to ensure that they would be ready if the French invaded. Societies like the United Englishmen had an inner, secret or 'private' committee, which met separately from the main club meetings, then reported back to the members at large. It was not easy for a spy to gain access to these committees until fully accepted and trusted by the other members. Once a spy had talked his way into a group, he could keep his employers fully briefed on events as they unfolded.

While Despard was in jail, at least two spies attended meetings of the United Englishmen, United Britons and other societies. One was John Tunbridge, a hairdresser who lived at No.3 Hare Walk, St Leonard's parish in Shoreditch. Tunbridge infiltrated a group called the Sons of Liberty, which had about sixty members and originally met at the White Hart in Long Alley, later moving to the Three Tuns in Whitechapel. The group's secretary, John Blythe, a shoemaker who lived in Bottle Alley, Bishopsgate Street, usually attended meetings 'armed with Pistols and a Knife', according to Tunbridge.

When Tunbridge joined, he was sounded out about his principles. Did he think that parliamentary reform was needed? When he answered in the affirmative, Tunbridge was sworn in and taught the secret signs to recognise other members: 'Put your Right Hand upon your left Elbow. Take off your Hat with both hands and in shaking hands to press your thumb upon the knuckle of the Fourth Finger.'[26]

The United Englishmen wanted the Sons of Liberty to join forces with them, perhaps because the arrests that spring had caused a drop in membership. 'Citizen Eastburn', a member of the UE, visited the Sons of Liberty 'to swear in such persons as were willing to join them.' Eastburn addressed them, saying that 'the Citizens had been asleep a long time, but now was the time to arise'. When he called those members who wanted to join the UE into a back room to be sworn in, Blythe, Mr Cooper (a schoolmaster), Cooper's son, and about twenty others took the secret oath one by one. In July the Sons of Liberty voted to become part of the United Englishmen.[27]

Eastburn told Tunbridge that the UE met at different places every week to avoid creating suspicion. Their previous meeting had been held at Bethnal Green, where they did 'their [military] Exercises in a Garden... and was [sic] instructed by a Serj't [sic] in the Guards'. When Tunbridge was sworn in, Eastburn explained that each man paid 'three pence down, and a halfpenny per Week for Arms and Ammunition'. Tunbridge asked him whether the society was flourishing, and Eastburn said 'they were never better supported...by the Great People'.

News of the Irish rebellion and the French invasion fleets caused great excitement in the secret societies that summer. At another meeting in July, 'Blyth[e] reported... that there were now '8,000 united Irishmen' in England.[28] A few days later, Eastburn said he had 'great news...there were 500 french soldiers landed in Ireland, wth 20,000 stand of arms...& that there would be 13,000 more land[ing] in Ireland which they would hear of very shortly; it was by the request of the committee of U.I. held in Paris!'

The revolutionists were keen to recruit more men to the cause. Soldiers and militia-men were prime targets because they had access to weapons. At the same meeting, Eastburn said there was a 'Prospect' of 'Friends' at Woolwich, where there was a garrison and arsenal. But recruits did not have to be soldiers; artizans and labourers would be useful, too. The Committee would select 'Single Men' to go from town to town 'to work at their Trades, & find out Men's Minds & form Divisions...about y^e [the] country.'

One of the members at this meeting was confused about what the leaders were discussing. Cooper junior asked Eastburn if the committee he had just mentioned was the same society that formed the United Englishmen. He said No, as 'they had had so many Traitors among them'.[29] Eastburn may have been referring to the United Britons.

The newly recruited United Englishmen took part in military training. Tunbridge discovered that each Division was to learn 'how to stop and face...a chief Thing for them to learn, and then they would easily learn to use the Firelock'. On the next Sunday, members were to meet at Hoxton Fields to practise drilling. However, Tunbridge's mission received a setback when he lost a show of hands to join the general committee. The news from Ireland was no longer so promising: 'They seemed low-spirited about Ireland, & thought they had been very much deceived.'[30]

While Tunbridge was busy with the UE, another spy, William Gent, attended meetings of the United Britons and the LCS. He believed that many groups were based in Spitalfields: 'I fear most of the Weavers who are out of work belong to these Societies'.[31] At the end of August he reported again: 'I have been very diligent in my enquiries...and have been pretty successful...I last night being Delegate joined the Committee of the London Corresponding Society held at the Crooked Billet Shire Lane Temple Bar, where Mr Eastbourne [Eastburn] was chosen their president and Mr Phillips their Secretary...I have been much in Company with Eastbourne, Blyth, Vaughan and others.'[32]

It was Gent who solved the mystery of the incriminating letter found in Father O'Coigley's pocket (as discussed in chapter 3). Several United Britons had visited Dr Crossfield in prison and Gent reported that he had 'heard something concerning Mr Coigley [sic]... concerning the Letter that was found in his Pocket, I learnt sufficient to know who was the author of it, which I believe to be Crossfield himself, as he said there was no one could come against him, that could testify to the writing of it, since Coigley was hanged and I rather think that Mr Coigley was Ignorant of its being in his Pocket when he was taken.'[33] (According to John Binns, O'Coigley had visited Dr Crossfield the night before he went to Margate).

Meanwhile, Tunbridge was still attending meetings of the UE. After news of a French landing in Ireland, another delegate, Cooper, said that 'a letter had been received from Scotland to the U.E. which stated there were several thousands ready for a little Diversion in Scotland if there were others ready (meaning England)'. But the hint was not received with enthusiasm by the UE members. A man called Price said cautiously, 'We are rather too weak to begin any Thing yet.'[34]

Some UE members had more immediate concerns, asking, for instance, how were their subscriptions being spent by the private (inner) committee? Cooper junior suggested they should stop paying in. Blythe tried to calm them down, saying that: 'They must never expect to know [how the money was spent] for the active Men were the whole of them all in danger of their lives if it was made public to the members. It was by that means that every former endeavour had been frustrated.' He reminded them of the 'Delegates that were taken at Margate.'[35] By late September, Tunbridge reported that membership of the group was tailing off, and the men were falling out amongst themselves. Some wanted to leave the UE and reform as the Sons of Liberty, their former incarnation.

In the meantime, Despard was moved from one prison to another. The government saw no immediate need to release those suspects now safely behind bars; it was busy dealing with the Irish rebellion. When Despard ended up in Coldbath Fields Prison (nicknamed the English Bastille), his devoted wife Catherine grew worried about his health. Despard's cell had no heat or light and he was living on bread and water. After complaining to the Home Office, with little effect, she contacted a hot-headed young politician, Sir Francis Burdett, who was making a name for himself.

Burdett (1770–1844) was educated at Westminster School and Oxford. He married a rich banker's daughter and first entered parliament in 1796, when he was elected MP for Boroughbridge in Yorkshire. A handsome, popular speaker, he was a determined opponent of the government's suspension of Habeas Corpus. He had some dealings with the United Irishmen – in 1798 Arthur O'Connor and John Binns had met at Burdett's house in Piccadilly. Sir Francis was also a member of the LCS, and so he was happy to visit Despard in prison.

Subsequently, Burdett put pressure on the prison authorities, and succeeded in getting the colonel moved to a better cell. Yet, despite his efforts on behalf of Despard and the other prisoners held without trial, Burdett was unable to get Habeas Corpus lifted.

Outlawed!

In the spring of 1799, the government's Committee of Secrecy used the spies' intelligence to publish a report on the United Englishmen, Irishmen and Scotsmen. These 'domestic traitors' had a 'systematic design' to overturn the 'laws, constitution, and government...in Great Britain and Ireland'.[36] Following these shock revelations, the government had no difficulty in persuading parliament to pass the Corresponding Societies Act, which outlawed all groups of this type, even peaceful corresponding societies. All Radical and democratic opposition groups were now banned.

The government was keen to crack down on democratic societies, not only because it feared that they were plotting revolution, but also because it knew that unrest was growing amongst the lower orders. This was a time of great hardship. The war with France, now in its sixth year, was increasingly unpopular with the lower classes. Food prices had gone through the roof, exacerbated by a bad harvest, and riots were breaking out in Britain's manufacturing districts. Ordinary people were more likely to join groups like the United Englishmen when their bellies were empty, unless deterred by severe penalties.

In May 1800, great alarm was felt when James Hatfield (or Hadfield), a former officer of the 15th Light Dragoons, fired a horse pistol at the box in which the King was seated in Drury Lane Theatre. The bullet missed the King, who remained calm, and Hatfield was grabbed by some members of the audience. When questioned, Hatfield denied that he had intended to kill the King; he explained that he was weary of life, and had hoped that the enraged theatre-goers would kill him. He denied belonging to the LCS, but his evidence was very incoherent. Hatfield had sustained a serious head injury while on active service in France, and in consequence had been discharged. He was tried for treason on 26 June 1800, but acquitted on grounds of insanity.

The Radicals and democrats enjoyed a brief respite when Pitt's government fell and Habeas Corpus was lifted at last. In March 1801, Despard and the other political prisoners breathed fresh air again. After what a contemporary biographer called Despard's 'long and cruel imprisonment',[37] it is unclear whether or not the colonel made the first approach to the surviving Irish and

English revolutionary cells, or vice versa. However, by the summer of 1802, the government was receiving intelligence on fresh United Britons and UE activity in London, Yorkshire and in Lancashire (where William Cheetham renewed his leadership of the United Englishmen).

However, one agent failed to obtain any useful information when he gate-crashed a meeting in the Stalybridge area. A Dukinfield magistrate wrote to the Home Secretary about a secret meeting at Buckton a few days earlier. (A large 'seditious' meeting at Buckton Castle had recently been dispersed by a troop of dragoons). At this small, local meeting the agent found about thirty men, 'all decently dressed...One of them made a particular sign to him with his hand...to know whether he knew ye Countersign. Finding that he did not answer they grew shy of saying anything that he could hear'.[38]

That August, problems arose at the London shipyards when the dockers went on strike for several weeks. Several prisoners broke out from the Woolwich prison hulks, too, but this trouble was quickly suppressed. These events may have been linked to Despard's United Britons, and an obscure Yorkshire group, who seemingly planned to rise up in concert with the United Britons and United Irishmen.

A Mysterious Yorkshire Plot

In the autumn, the Home Office sent former soldier Thomas Hirst to the North, 'for the purpose of discovering the plans of the disaffected'. From Leeds, Hirst sent a long, rambling reports of a secret meeting with some men near Wakefield, during which he had heard rumours about a 'Major General Desport' [sic] of the 'Directory', a mysterious group which communicated with Ireland and Scotland. Hirst claimed that such august personages as the Duke of Norfolk, Sir Francis Burdett, and prominent Whigs like Charles James Fox and Charles Grey were involved with the Directory. They planned something big for the opening of parliament, he warned: 'I don't know what will be to do when Parliament meets but I think som[e]thing.'[39] Thomas also wrote that he feared for his life if his spying activities were discovered.

The local magistrates were initially very reluctant to forward Hirst's reports to London. As Earl Fitzwilliam said, they found it difficult to believe him, as Hirst's letters 'implicated so many respectable names'. (Fitzwilliam, the former Lord Lieutenant of Ireland, was then the West Riding's Lord Lieutenant.) The Earl believed that Hirst was 'a most consummate rascal, a fellow of as bad a character as can be found…He has been once tried for a capital offence, & though he escaped conviction, there was no doubt about his guilt'.[40]

Nevertheless, Earl Fitzwilliam asked the magistrates to forward Hirst's information to the Home Office, but he warned the current Home Secretary, Lord Pelham, about the spy's unreliable character. Despite Fitzwilliam's misgivings, he felt that Hirst should be allowed to continue spying:

> *'Worthless as he may be, he may not be the worse Agent, for the purposes of getting into the secrets of the Disaffected, if there are any Combinations of Men, for purposes dangerous to Government. The Magistrates will be always on their guard against acting upon information given by him, unless corroborated by other circumstances. The only mischief…will be the few guineas that he will squeeze out of the* [Home] *Office, for his pretended services.'*[41]

Something was definitely afoot in Yorkshire, however, because arms were discovered, and secret oaths were being taken. William Simnet, a collier from Birley Hollins in Sheffield, later testified to the magistrates that between September and Christmas of 1801, a man called William Ronksley had repeatedly asked him to join a Society 'to reduce the Price of Bread'. Ronksley (Ronkesley) later admitted that its true aim 'was to raise a disturbance in the Nation'. When Simnet joined the society, he learned that it planned to 'take the Barracks' when ordered by its 'Chiefs and Conductors'.

Simnet, his brother Edward, and Ronksley went to William Lee's house near New Church, Sheffield, where they were sworn in using an oath printed on paper. After repeating the words of the oath, Lee gave Simnet the paper to kiss. This group used the same secret oath as the United Britons.

In early August 1802 (about the time of the London dockers' strike and the prisoners' escape), Ronksley told Simnet that 'orders were come that all the Members of the Society were to arm themselves'. Ronskley asked a whitesmith (tinplate worker) at Grindle Gate to make some arms, which were buried in a wood soon afterwards, when the group became unnerved by the failure of the breakout at the Woolwich hulks. When this collection of arms was dug up after Simnet's arrest, it included seven large spear heads, and 'large pieces of steel made sharp, in the state they come from the grinder before being cut into files'.

When Ronksley was charged with illegal oath-taking, he tried to put a brave face on it. He told local magistrate Hugh Parker: 'When the Arms were taken to be buried, he intended them to remain there for ever…the Arms were brought to his house when he was from home…he never took an Oath in his Life, or ever offered to give one to any Person.'[42] Ronksley and Lee were lucky to get away with a sentence of seven years' transportation.

Despard's Downfall

Back in London, a Home Office agent called Moody, who had previously acted as a government mole in the LCS, kept watch on Despard and the United Britons. An embittered soldier in the 3rd Grenadier Guards, Thomas Windsor, was also sending information to the Home Department, hoping for a reward. The spies reported that the rebels hoped to recruit hundreds of the soldiers now stationed in the capital to form a revolutionary army, and Despard was seemingly in charge of this task. As described earlier, the plan was for joint uprisings to take place in England and Ireland, and Despard was in contact with United Irishman William Dowdall. War with France was expected to recommence very soon.

Some soldiers who had joined the United Britons were itching for the rising to begin, and Despard was struggling to keep them in check. According to another soldier, Thomas Blades, several United Britons met at the Bleeding Heart, Hatton Garden around 13 September, including John Francis, Charles Pendrill, and MacNamara, an Irishman. One of the men at the gathering, Wratten, wanted to know when they would move into action. Charles Pendrill burst out angrily: 'The attack would have taken place before, if it had not been for two or three cowards'. Pendrill claimed he could 'bring a thousand men into the field at any time,' and if 'he saw any of them shew the least symptom of cowardice he would blow his brains out.'

Francis also wanted the attack to take place soon, before the 'Den of Thieves' (parliament) met. If the government discovered their plans, then it would take steps to ensure they could not meet or contact one another any more. Pendrill declared, 'There was not the least danger of it ever being found out, for he had belonged to it a considerable time, and many persons had been taken up [arrested] at different times, but had never divulged the secret.' If anyone betrayed them, Pendrill threatened, 'he should have a dagger in his breast directly.'[43]

Despard and the United Britons planned to attack multiple targets in the capital. They would seize the Bank of England, the Tower of London and the armouries (and the weapons stored there), make 'Insurrection Rebellion and War' on the kingdom, and kill the King. As a sign to encourage fellow rebels to rise up, the mail-coaches would be prevented from leaving London.[44]

Spy Thomas Windsor kept the Home Office informed via Mr Bownas, an army agent. When he alerted them that a meeting was planned at the Oakley Arms public house in Lambeth, the government pounced. Despard and almost forty conspirators – mostly labourers and soldiers, many of them Irish – were arrested when they met on 16 November 1802.

To his contemporaries, Despard's mixing with the lower orders was suspicious in itself. As the attorney general commented at his trial, why would a man of 'birth, education, genteel manners, and of rank in the army…associate with the lowest of mankind', unless he was up to no good?[45] Two days later, Despard, fettered with irons, was questioned by the Privy Council at Lord Pelham's office for two-and-a-half hours, then sent to Newgate Prison.

On 25 January the following year, Despard and his fellow prisoners were tried for high treason by a Special Commission at the Sessions House (next to Horsemonger Lane Gaol) in Newington, Surrey. They all pleaded 'not guilty'. As well as conspiring to kill the King, the defendants were charged with seducing (i.e. subverting) soldiers and sailors from their duty, and other 'liege subjects' with the aim of imprisoning, or deposing the King. Thomas Windsor claimed that Despard had said that the people of Leeds, Sheffield and Birmingham were ripe for rebellion, and that he had exclaimed, 'If nobody else will do it, I will do it myself! I have weighed the matter well, and my heart is callous!'[46]

The conspirators were charged with administering illegal oaths to soldiers. The secret oath of the United Britons was found on a printed card:

'CONSTITUTION!

'The independence of Great Britain and Ireland – an equalization of civil,
political, and religious rights – an ample provision for the widows of the
heroes who shall fall in the contest – a liberal reward for distinguished merit.
These are the objects for which we contend; and to obtain these objects we
swear to be united.

'In the awful presence of Almighty God, I, A.B. [the oath-taker's
name] *do voluntarily declare, that I will endeavour, to the utmost of my*
power, to obtain the object of this union; namely, to recover those rights
which the Supreme Being, in his infinite bounty has given to all men; that
neither hopes, nor fears, rewards, nor punishments, shall ever induce me to
give any information, directly or indirectly, concerning the business, or of
any member of this or any similar society, so help me God.'[47]

Throughout his trial, Despard refused to incriminate anyone else and he
maintained a 'firm and manly deportment', taking notes of the evidence
against him as the trial progressed.[48] As the main evidence against the
colonel was from informers like Blades and Windsor, contemporaries like
the Radical politician Henry Hunt believed that Despard was stitched up by
the government.

Despard's former fellow officer Lord Nelson (then famous for his naval
successes against the French and their allies) appeared as a character witness
on his behalf, but to no avail. On 19 February, Despard and nine of the
defendants were found guilty. The jury recommended Despard to mercy
because of his former good behaviour and conduct. Nevertheless, Despard
and Wood, Broughton, Francis, Wratten, Graham and MacNamara were
all sentenced to be hanged by the neck, 'but not till you are quite dead;
then to be cut down, your bowels taken out, and cast into the fire before
your faces; your heads to be taken off, and your bodies quartered.'[49] Despard
listened coolly to his death sentence and bowed to the court as he left.
The prisoners' sentences were later commuted to hanging, followed by
beheading. (This would be the last time this sentence for treason was passed
by an English court.)

Because the government had 'jumped the gun' and arrested Despard and
his confederates, it missed the opportunity to discover the conspiracy's true

extent. After the arrests, a Yorkshire magistrate wrote to Earl Fitzwilliam to inform him that secret meetings were still taking place:

> *'There is no doubt of a numerous midnight meeting having been held at Stay Bridge; and that many new members were sworn into the Society... The women all talk misteriously* [sic]. *There is a general expectation of they know not what. Like the second advent – the day is coming – the Day is at hand. And I have no doubt that if Despard & his party had discovered themselves in London in numbers, there w*^d *have been a general Rebellion against superiors throughout the country.'*[50]

Those rebels still at large may have considered themselves safe at this point, as they had avoided arrest. The French and Irish continued making preparations for insurrection, culminating in Robert Emmet's disastrous Dublin uprising in 1803.

The day before his execution, Despard had a last, awful meeting with his wife Caroline, then fell asleep. He awoke at about eight in the evening, and one of the prison officers reported hearing him exclaim: 'Me – they shall receive no information from me – no! not for all the gifts, the gold, and the jewels, in possession of the crown.'[51]

Despard and his accomplices were executed on 21 February 1803. The colonel remained resolute to the last, and when asked by the chaplain to recite the Lord's Prayer, he refused. Despard gave a farewell speech on the scaffold in which he reiterated his innocence:

> *'His Majesty's ministers know as well as I do that I am not guilty, yet they avail themselves of a legal pretext to destroy a man, because he has been a friend to truth, to liberty, to justice* [here the section of the crowd nearest to him gave a huge cheer]...*because he has been a friend to the poor and oppressed. But citizens, I hope and trust, notwithstanding my fate, and the fate of those who no doubt will soon follow me, that the principles of freedom, of humanity, and of justice, will finally triumph over falsehood, tyranny, and delusion.'*

He concluded by wishing his 'fellow citizens...all health, happiness, and freedom, which I have endeavoured, as far as was in my power, to procure for you, and for mankind in general'.[52]

Somewhere in the immense crowd gathered to watch Despard's final agonies was Jeremiah Brandreth, a framework-knitter from Nottingham. Did Brandreth have a premonition that one day he would meet the same fate?

Chapter Five

S is for Spy

Despard was dead. The failure of Robert Emmet's Dublin insurrection put the final nail in the coffin of the United Irishmen's dreams. The great blaze of revolutionary ferment ignited by the French Revolution appeared to be extinguished.

All seemed quiet for a few years, but discontent bubbled beneath the surface. Workers in Britain's great manufacturing heartlands faced an unprecedented squeeze on their living standards. When the hardship caused by low wages was compounded by high food prices, the authorities knew that trouble loomed. The years 1811–1813 were dominated by major threats to the King's peace: the Luddites. Nottinghamshire, Lancashire, and the West Riding of Yorkshire were the main flashpoints of Luddite activity, although there were outbreaks elsewhere.

The war against Bonaparte had led to the loss of foreign markets and a British trade slump. Poor harvests also pushed food prices through the roof. In the summer of 1812, the residents of Bolton in Lancashire sent an address containing an impassioned plea for peace to the Prince Regent. (The Prince of Wales had become Regent on 5 February, owing to a severe recurrence of George III's illness). Bolton's 'loyal and industrious workers' had seen prices double over the last few months, but their wages had fallen to a quarter of pre-war rates. They begged the Prince Regent's sympathy for their 'pale and ghastly countenances – their squalid and ragged clothing – their houses emptied of furniture – their half-starved and half-fed children crying for bread, or begging with piteous moan from door to door for the dole of charity'. Would 'the most glorious results of war, and victory abroad… be sufficient to compensate for the mass of wretchedness at home'?[1] But the war against France dragged on and on.

An Assassin Strikes

There was shocking proof of the people's hatred of the government that May, when Prime Minister Spencer Perceval was shot through the heart. The assassin, John Bellingham, was already well-known to the Home Office. A Liverpool merchant, Bellingham had tried to gain redress for years from the government for an unjust spell of imprisonment by the Russian authorities he had suffered while working in St Petersburg. A few weeks before the murder, Bellingham had written to the Bow Street magistrates to warn that if his requests were still ignored, then he would 'feel justified in executing justice myself'. The government could move quickly when it wanted to: Bellingham was tried, convicted and hanged in just seven days.

When the news of Perceval's assassination reached Nottingham, its citizens celebrated. 'The bells were rung, bonfires were lighted, and a tumultuous crowd of people assembled...with drums beating' and 'flags flying'.[2]

Nottinghamshire was famous for making cotton and silk stockings (framework knitting), as well as lace. Violent protests had previously achieved better piece rates for the local framework knitters: in 1779 over 300 stocking-frames were smashed and a house torched in Nottingham, after parliament refused to set a fair minimum wage. The masters backed down and agreed reasonable wages, and peace reigned once more.

The Nottinghamshire Luddites

When trouble flared again in Nottinghamshire during 1811, the framework knitters were fighting new cheap and nasty stockings, known as 'cut-ups', which had swamped the trade. (Luddite violence was not necessarily a reaction against new machinery; activists took pride in their craftsmanship and wanted to keep standards high). 'Cut-ups' were made on long-established 'wide frames' formerly used for making pantaloons, which were now unfashionable. Cloth made on these frames was 'cut-up' into pieces, then sewn together to make items like stockings or socks, but these soon fell to pieces (because they were not knitted in one piece, cut-ups unravelled). Many small master manufacturers lost trade because of these shoddy articles, too, as customers did not want to pay the higher prices asked for quality goods.

In November 1811, a furious mob broke up stocking and lace frames at Sutton-in-Ashfield. Next, employers making cut-ups, or paying poor piece rates, received threatening letters warning them to dismantle their machines or risk a visit from 'Ned Ludd' and friends. According to legend, Ned Ludd was a young apprentice framework knitter from Sherwood Forest who had defiantly smashed a knitting frame when he fell out with his master. The name General Ludd, or variants thereof, was swiftly adopted by workers in several counties as a bogeyman to frighten their 'betters'.[3]

Knitting-frames, rented from masters, were scattered in workers' houses or small workshops, which made them easy targets. The Luddites travelled swiftly from one village to another at night, smashed the machines, then melted away into the darkness. Frame-breaking was made a capital offence, but the attacks continued. Nearly 100 frames were destroyed during the last week of January 1812, and Nottinghamshire's wealthier inhabitants must have felt under siege, wondering who would be attacked next.

At this time, the Nottinghamshire Luddites' motives appear to have been purely economic, not political, but the authorities did not know that. Whitehall received letter after letter from anxious magistrates who were convinced that an armed insurrection was imminent. On 22 March, a letter was forwarded to the Home Office in which a Nottingham gentleman claimed that '17,000 committed men...involved in the present system of outrage' were busy 'procuring arms'. He believed that the Luddites were in contact with Yorkshire and Lancashire workers and weapons were being made for them.[4]

The magistrates made huge efforts to discover whether or not a single leader was masterminding the frame-breaking. A prominent wage-campaigner, Gravenor Henson, was suspected but the authorities could not obtain any worthwhile information implicating him or others. The Luddites they captured refused to talk. For instance, at Leicester the Treasury Solicitor interrogated convicted Luddite William Quenby, while he was awaiting transportation aboard one of the prison hulks. 'He has either no Information to communicate, or...is determined to with:hold [sic] it'; the solicitor 'could get nothing from him' about his Luddite comrades. Quenby had been convicted on the evidence of an informer, Sarah Hickling, who received a £50 reward.[5]

The government flooded the Nottingham area with troops and frame-breaking died down again, although there were fresh outbreaks in late 1812.

'Enoch Shall Smash Them'

Meanwhile, news of frame-breaking had reached the West Riding, where many people were starving, too. In Yorkshire the Luddites mostly came from the ranks of the 'croppers' or 'shear-men', highly skilled workers who cropped the 'nap' (raised fibres) on woollen cloth by hand. They used immensely large, heavy shears to give cloth a smooth, dense finish. New 'shearing-frames' speeded up this process, which meant less work was available for hand croppers. In February 1812, shearing-frames and other machines were smashed in the Huddersfield and Spen Valley areas. A £200 reward was offered for information leading to the successful conviction of the Luddites responsible.

Initially, no one was hurt during the Yorkshire attacks: the Luddites' wrath was reserved for the machines. The great hammer the Luddites used to break the machines was nick-named 'Enoch', as the first shearing-frames had been built in Marsden by tool-maker Enoch Taylor. The Luddites said 'Enoch has made them and Enoch shall smash them', and commemorated its deeds in song:

> 'Great Enoch still shall lead the van
> Stop him who dare! Stop him who can!
> Press forward every gallant man
> With hatchet, pike and gun!
> Oh, the cropper lads for me,
> The gallant lads for me,
> Who with lusty stroke
> The shear frames broke,
> The cropper lads for me!'[6]

By now the Yorkshire mill-owners were furious about the Luddite attacks. Two spirited manufacturers, William Cartwright of Rawfolds near Cleckheaton, and William Horsfall of Ottiwells, were determined to defend their property. They defied the Luddites to do their worst, armed their workforce and barricaded their mills. Horsfall even acquired a cannon, vowing to ride up to his saddle-girths in Luddite blood if necessary.

George Mellor, a cropper, was one of the most prominent Luddites in the Spen Valley area of West Yorkshire. Mellor worked at John Wood's cropping shop near Longroyd Bridge, Huddersfield. Shortly before midnight on Saturday, 11 April 1812, over 100 Luddites led by Mellor marched silently towards Cartwright's mill at Rawfolds. The men carried guns, pistols, cudgels, and huge hammers. Their faces were disguised with masks or blackened; some wore women's clothing. The mill was in darkness as they approached and the two sentries at the mill-gates were swiftly overpowered. As the men's hammers shattered the gates, Cartwright and his men, who were concealed inside, greeted them with a volley of deadly fire.

The Luddites returned fire, but the mill was too heavily fortified and they retreated. Two mortally wounded men, John Booth and Samuel Hartley, were left behind. Tradition has it that Cartwright refused them medical assistance, then relented when an angry crowd of locals gathered. The wounded Luddites were carried to a nearby inn. Aqua fortis (nitric acid – a corrosive liquid) was used on the dying men, possibly in a clumsy attempt by doctors to cauterize their wounds – or maybe to cause pain, in the hope that the men would betray their friends.

The Reverend Hammond Roberson, a local clergyman, is said to have repeatedly hounded the two men to talk. At last Booth, realizing he was about to die, beckoned Roberson to his side: 'Can you keep a secret?' he whispered. 'I can!' Roberson reassured him. 'So can I,' said Booth, and died. His friend Hartley died some hours later; he took the Luddites' secrets with him to the grave, too.[7]

The Yorkshire Luddites vowed to avenge their comrades. The following week, William Cartwright narrowly escaped death when two men fired at him. Their identities were never discovered. Then on 28 April, Cartwright's fellow mill-owner William Horsfall was shot dead on Crosland Moor by George Mellor, Benjamin Walker and two accomplices. They swore an oath on the Bible never to reveal who had taken part in the murder.

For several months, it proved impossible for the authorities to discover any decent leads on the Yorkshire Luddites. Ordinary folk remained loyal to them, despite their violence, as they knew that the men's families were destitute. Some may also have feared reprisals from the Luddites, if they betrayed them to the authorities.

Trouble Looms in the North-West

While the authorities hunted the Nottingham and Yorkshire Luddites, north-west England also witnessed outbreaks of violence as cotton workers faced starvation.

The handloom weavers had seen an unprecedented drop in their piecework rates. The fall in earnings was owing to complex economic factors including foreign competition, and an influx of migrant workers from rural areas and Ireland.

The weavers, however, believed there was an obvious culprit for their lack of earning power. They blamed the recently introduced powerlooms - machines powered by water or steam which wove cloth more quickly and cheaply than even the most industrious weaver. Powerlooms required major capital investment, and at this date they produced poor quality cloth, so they were not yet widely used by manufacturers. However, the handloom weavers were determined to prevent this potential threat to their livelihoods from spreading further.

The cotton districts had a history of industrial unrest. During 1808–1809, the cotton weavers of England and Scotland petitioned parliament to set a minimum wage, but parliament refused to intervene. At that date, the prevailing wisdom was that state interference with any industry would have a disastrous effect on jobs. The Lancashire weavers went on strike for several weeks in late May 1808 after their appeals to parliament achieved nothing. Their bosses were forced to make concessions and increase their wages.

An embryonic trade union movement had grown up in the north-west, according to the Glasgow weaver and spy, Alexander Richmond. 'Central committees' of delegates from several districts were formed in 'Manchester, Bolton, Preston, Carlisle, etc.', with links to groups in Ireland and Scotland (see chapter 9).[8] The Lancashire weavers' meetings were far more likely to have been attempts to organize and improve wages than to plan revolution. However, as unions were banned by the Combination Acts, it was difficult for spies – some of whom were not exactly well-educated – to distinguish between unions, parliamentary reform groups, and revolutionary organizations, especially when all these societies were illegal.

By 1812 hunger had made the weavers desperate and they were ready to lash out against the hated powerlooms. Lancashire weavers were no strangers to direct action; twenty years earlier, Luddites had burned down Grimshaw's powerloom factory at Manchester. (The machines at this mill had been designed by Edmund Cartwright, the brother of Major Cartwright, the parliamentary reformer, which may partly explain the Major's abhorrence of violence).

In early March, Charles Prescot, a Stockport rector and magistrate, forwarded information he had received from an impoverished weaver to the Home Office. Stockport, in Cheshire, was then an important centre for powerloom weaving. The weaver, who had asked to remain anonymous for his own safety, told Prescot that:

'Several weavers…are determined to do away with those Steam Looms… there is [sic] *45,000 that is suffering by it besides other Trades. They are entirely worn out'.*

The men felt that even if peace was suddenly declared, they would be no better off unless the powerlooms were removed. Weavers from different districts were in contact with one another, and 'The 45,000 cou'd [sic] all rise in one night and wou'd [sic] do if they have not redress…The whole country is dissatisfied. A Man's life is of no value – I have five children and a Wife, the children are all under 8 years of age.'

The weaver earned a net wage of nine shillings per week after deductions, 'and I work sixteen hours a day to get that – But there are thousands that do not get 8s per week'. The family spent two shillings per week on coal, and one shilling per week on candles, leaving them just six shillings to feed seven people; they could not afford to buy bread. 'My family live upon potatoes chiefly and we have one pint of milk per day,' the weaver claimed.[9]

The weavers were not the only members of the lower classes affected by high prices and food shortages. During April, food riots broke out in Manchester, but the disturbances were swiftly put down by yeomanry cavalry and troops. Colliers and other workers were amongst the angry mobs, and the Manchester Exchange building was damaged in one of these incidents. In the same month, several powerloom factories came under attack. A mob

at least 2,000-strong assailed Daniel Burton's mill at Middleton, and Wroe
and Duncough's mill at Westhoughton was destroyed. Mill-owners' homes
in Stockport were assaulted by rioters led 'by two men, dressed in women's
clothes, who were called General Ludd's wives'.[10]

However, the story of the north-west cotton districts in 1812 is not easy to
unravel. The picture is complicated by agents provocateurs, who incited the
weavers to break the law – and risk their necks. They found a ready audience
amongst men with hungry mouths to feed.

Colonel Ralph Fletcher of Bolton, one of the biggest spymasters in the
area, was already monitoring the weavers' and Radicals' activities through
his extensive (and expensive) spy network. His spies included John Bent, a
cotton dealer, alias 'B', and a father-and-son team, Simon (Simeon) and John
Stones. Stones junior did not report directly to Fletcher; he was supervised
by Captain Warr, an adjutant in the local militia, who wrote down his reports
and sent them to Fletcher. Stones was referred to as '/S/' in Warr's reports,
and his father as 'Old /S/'.

Colonel Fletcher wrote to the Home Office in late March 1812 to warn
that delegates from Nottingham had been in the Bolton area. An adjutant
from the local militia had sent a spy to attend the nightly meetings, but
Fletcher also wanted guidance – should he arrest the delegates and break up
these meetings? If he did so, he risked jeopardizing the identity of his spies,
especially if they were required to testify against the Luddites. Fletcher was
advised not to 'take any step which would have the effect of interrupting
the Channel of Information...of the meetings of the Disaffected in the
neighbourhood of Bolton...you should...pursue the same course of silent
& private observation.' If 'anything material' transpired, then Fletcher must
inform the Home Office and await further instructions. It is clear that the
authorities wished to avoid unrest, as the Home Secretary, Mr Ryder, added
that he hoped that 'the vigilance of the Civil Officers...aided by the military'
would prevent 'any open acts of Violence' in the area.[11]

At first the Home Office seemed happy with Fletcher's spy ring. Under-
Secretary Beckett wrote to Fletcher that: 'You seem to be furnished with
pretty accurate information' about the 'nightly meetings', which had taken
place earlier that month. He asked Fletcher to warn any persons whose
property was likely to be attacked, whilst ensuring he kept his sources 'as

Map of England and Wales, Henry Fisher, 1823. *Author's collection*

Seamen complain about their rations prior to the mutiny at the Nore. Cassell's *Illustrated History of England Vol. VI.* (Cassell, Petter and Galpin, c.1864)

Noted Radicals: John Wilkes, John Horne Tooke, Sir Francis Burdett (5th Baronet), William Cobbett and Henry Hunt. *History of England*, Henry Fisher, Son, & Co., 1828. *Author's collection*

'True reform of parliament, or Patriots lighting a revolutionary bonfire'. Sir Frances Burdett, the central figure, waves a red cap of liberty while Horne Tooke sets fire to a mass of papers, and an angry mob attacks parliament. James Gillray, 1809. *Courtesy Library of Congress, LC-DIG-ds-01039*

Coldbath Fields Gaol, *The Newgate Calendar Vol. III*, London, n.d., c.1820. Col. Despard wa[s] imprisoned here without trial in 1798. The Cato St conspirators were held here in 1820 before bein[g] sent to the Tower of London. *Author's collection*

Plan of the City of Westminster, published by Cowie and Strange. Whitehall, where the Home Offic[e] was based, is approximately centre right. Thomas Allen's *History of London*, George Virtue, 1829[.] *Author's collection*

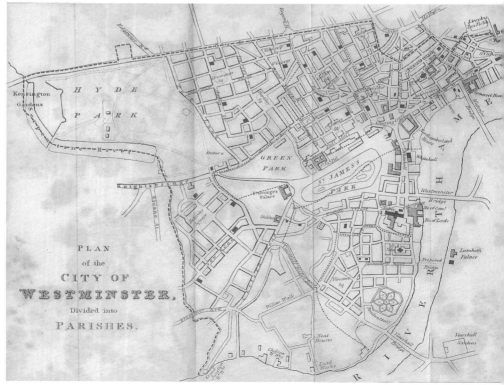

A 'Charley' is teased by a Regency buck. Nightwatchmen like these were not very effective guardians of law and order. George and Robert Cruikshank, *Life in London*, John Camden Hotten, Piccadilly, 1869. *Author's collection*

The Borough of Southwark, divided into parishes. The Oakley Arms pub, where Despard and his accomplices were arrested, was on Oakley Street (far left of map), off Waterloo Rd. Horsemonger Lane Gaol, where Despard was imprisoned and executed, is marked as the 'County Jaol [sic]' just off Newington Causeway. Thomas Allen's *History of London*, George Virtue, 1829. *Author's collection*

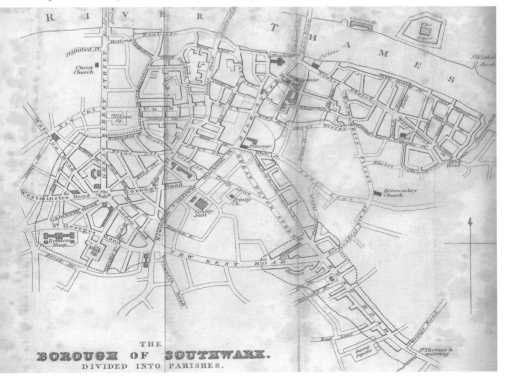

Alfoxton (Alfoxden) House. The poet William Wordsworth was staying here with his sister Dorothy in 1797, when he and Samuel Taylor Coleridge were suspected of being spies for the French. © *Sue Wilke*

Copenhagen House, circa 1800. The London Corresponding Society held rallies near here in the 1790s. *Old and New London* Vol. II. (Cassell, Petter & Galpin, c.1890). *Author's collection*

Map of Ireland, 1806. *Barclay's Dictionary*, c.1813. *Author's Collection*

CITIZEN M.C.BROWNE.

Delegate from the SHEFFIELD & LEEDS Const.! Soc.?
to the British Convention.

Citizen Matthew Campbell Browne, 'Delegate from the Sheffield & Leeds Constitutional Societies to the British Convention' at Edinburgh in 1794. Engraving by John Kay, 1794. Browne was the editor of the *Patriot* newspaper. Hugh Paton (ed.), *A Series of Original Portraits and Caricature Etchings by the late John Kay*, Vol. 2, (Adam and Charles Black, 1877). *Author's collection*